2023
CHRISTMAS
with
Southern Living

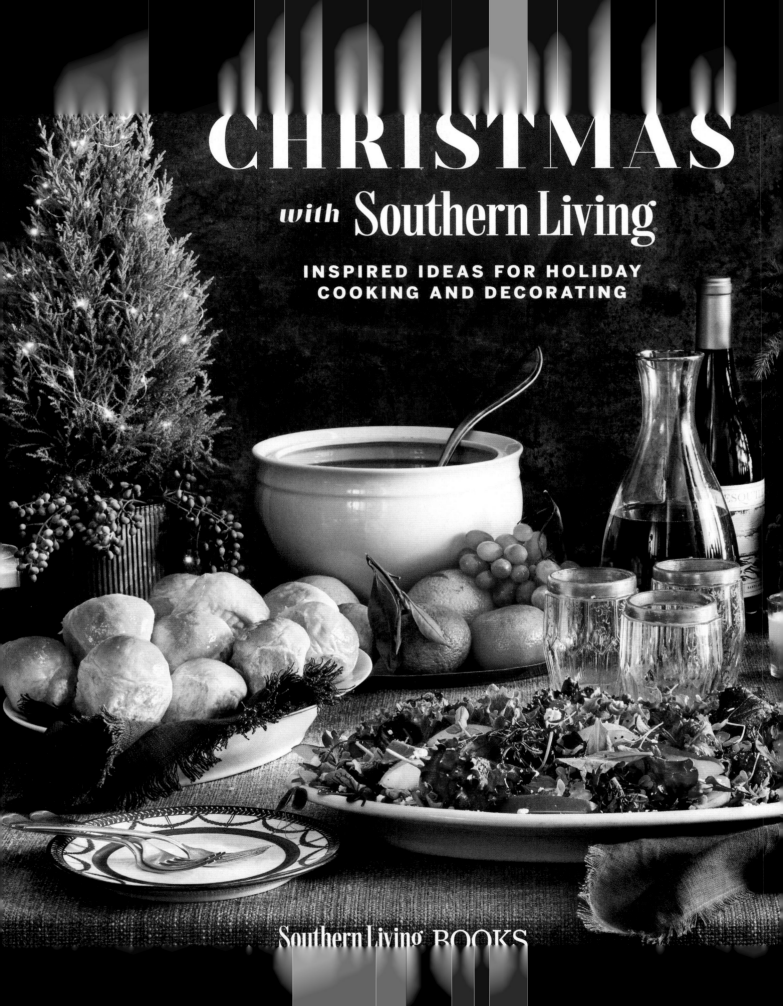

CHRISTMAS
with Southern Living

INSPIRED IDEAS FOR HOLIDAY COOKING AND DECORATING

Southern Living BOOKS

CONTENTS

CONTENTS 4
WELCOME LETTER 9

DECORATE 10
ENTERTAIN 56
SAVOR & SHARE 104

RESOURCES 169
GENERAL INDEX 170
METRIC EQUIVALENTS 172
RECIPE INDEX 173
HOLIDAY PLANNER 177

The architectural symmetry of this striking stone home lends itself to repeating elements—large wreaths, rich red bows, and graceful waves of garland—for a beautifully balanced display that stops passersby.

The holidays are here again!

Of course, we've been decking halls, cooking Christmas feasts, and whipping up batch after batch of cookies since our lawns were green and cicadas still hummed. Our team's planning and preparation for this book starts at the first blush of summer. From brainstorming sessions and prop-buying trips to menu-planning and recipe development, the edition you hold is the culmination of an annual team effort that's been on auto-repeat for over four decades. We hope you find as much inspiration and joy in the following pages as we do in the process of making the book.

Thanks to the *Southern Living* kitchen staff, food stylists, prop stylists, and photographers who make sure that each recipe tastes and looks delicious and that every table setting is festive. And cheers to the location stylists who generously opened their doors to share their unique holiday traditions and personal approaches to holiday decorating.

May this merry season bring you much comfort and joy!

Katherine Cobbs
EXECUTIVE EDITOR

1

Decorate

HOLIDAY LOOKBOOK

HOLIDAYS
with Southern

Our stylists invite us inside to see how they

AT HOME
Living Stylists

deck their halls at home for the holidays.

Hark, the Sorbet Colors Sing!

LINDSEY BEATTY has used her creative talents to set the scene on dozens of photo shoots during her decades-long career as a decorating editor and prop stylist for national magazines. When not on the clock producing a story, she brings her love for bold prints and juicy palettes to client homes, a beach vacation rental, and her family's residence. Not one to shy away from layering color, pattern, texture, and finishes, Lindsey's Christmas decorating style proves that a nontraditional approach can be the merriest of all.

"My jumping-off point for holiday decorating is always the room.
I like to work with the existing décor and think of the holiday
layer as if I'm accessorizing a room any other time of year."

As former style director of *Southern Living* and *Coastal Living*, it's no surprise that Lindsey's style is a marriage of the South and the coast. "I like colorful, breezy spaces with a dose of tradition and elegance—think Palm Beach meets New Orleans. I love anything rattan, but I also love Louis XVI." For Lindsey, it's all about the mix, which also applies to her holiday decorating. "I'm a maximalist and love a collected, personal look." She pairs Royal Crown Derby Gold Aves salad plates from her wedding registry, gold bamboo flatware purchased on eBay, and green goblets from the Goodwill store with woven lemon napkin rings for elegant high-low flair. "With so much greenery in the house, a floral centerpiece feels unnecessary. So instead, I went with funky Anthro candlesticks and simply twirled a garland down the table to make it more holiday. Other than that, I'd repeat this table setting any time of year."

> "Once I started layering color and pattern, it became a 'more is more' situation—a theory I also apply to holiday decorating."

Holiday Punch

A wife and mom of three boys, Lindsey's style evolved with her growing family. When the boys were toddlers, she traded an all-white décor for one filled with striking patterns and juicy colors for durability. "I temper the craziness with solids and grasscloth, so it's less Barbie dreamhouse," she says with a laugh. The bare wood of the whitewashed dining table keeps things casual. It provides a blank canvas for a layered holiday setting minus worry over spills or stained linens. A white lacquered console enlisted for bar service is equally forgiving. "I try not to be too matchy-matchy to keep things from looking formulaic," she admits.

Room to Play

Flea market finds and performance fabrics on furnishings mean nothing is too precious. "We've had a few casualties due to flying footballs, spilled Gatorades, and general raucousness, but I don't get worked up when accidents happen. My boys are jaded by all the pink—it's a neutral to them now. Luckily, my husband is on board."

Lindsey admits that in her decades of work, she's easily decorated a Christmas tree every month of the year. Her kids don't raise eyebrows if she's gift-wrapping empty boxes in May or pulling out ornaments in July. However, when the first of December rolls around, that's her cue for decking Beatty halls. She always puts a tree in the front window for curb appeal. "I love the whimsical look of a silver-tipped fir, though lighting them takes finesse. Florists wire is a great way to attach the lights to the branches and hide the cords, so you don't lose the tree's open, airy habit. That way, the ornaments stand out in the gaps between the branches. Lots of ribbons cascading down the tree are a must!" She tucks Shiny Brite ornaments inside the lanterns above the fireplace for shimmer and beefs up an evergreen garland with eucalyptus and Italian Ruscus for interest that holds up well for weeks.

Making Spirits Bright

Lindsey hosts family on Christmas Eve, so she adds holiday touches to every room and includes a flocked tree in the breakfast room because guests always gather near the kitchen. "I had to exercise restraint with the Bubble Glass ornaments. I rarely use just one type of ornament on a tree, but anything else would detract here." Not one to use fake flowers, she is not opposed to faux Christmas trees. "I love a flocked tree, but a real one is too messy." A champagne station keeps minglers merry next to the tree, and a table is set for overflow guests. In the kitchen, a few holiday accents draw the eye as guests fill plates with food or cups with eggnog.

"Growing up, we spent Christmas with my grandparents in Eufaula, Alabama. Grandmother Momoo always made eggnog and gave everyone a task. If you folded the egg whites too aggressively, failed to beat the yolks long enough, or poured the whiskey in too fast, she was quick to correct!" The family eggnog is fluffy and cloudlike, so folding or stirring deflates it. "We like to pile scoops of ice cream in a glass and dollop the eggnog on top. It's divine, and I've never had another eggnog quite like it."

"Our schedule is so
hectic most of the year, so
I really try to cocoon
a bit during the holidays to
reflect on what's been and
what's to come."

Rest Ye Merrymakers

"My prop closet is always brimming and can get unruly. But
during the holidays, I look at it as an abundance of riches. I
have saved so many Christmas props and decorative pieces
for future shoots that I have plenty of accents to weave into
every room of our house. Frankly, I'd run out of places to put
things if some of it didn't trickle into our bedrooms!" Lindsey
exclaims. Little nods to the season—like a mini tree, wreaths
above a headboard and sink, and pom-pom garland here and
there—add to the main suite's ambience with little effort. "I
figure it's better used and enjoyed than relegated to a closet,"
she admits.

All-Star Accents

Longtime readers of Southern Living know BUFFY HARGETT'S work. As a senior photo stylist for decades, she is an expert decorator of Christmas trees and mantels. She has easily strung miles of garlands and string lights and has creatively wrapped more presents than Santa's elves combined. Beyond the holidays, from container gardens and centerpieces to tablescapes and home interiors, Buffy produces an array of beautiful vignettes for the magazine's glossy pages throughout the year. When not on set, she is known for the breathtakingly gorgeous floral installations she creates for weddings and special events. During the busy holiday season, Buffy keeps the decorating simple at home. She shows how small-scale accents can be big on wow factor.

B

Buffy Hargett describes her style as simple and organic with twists on traditional. Creativity runs her family. "My mother, an avid gardener, artist, interior and floral designer, taught me everything I know," Buffy says. That includes incorporating nature's elements into her home's décor throughout the year, but more so during the holidays, when greenery greets you right at the front door.

"Wait until a week or so into December to start your decorating, and your fresh greenery will last right through the holidays."

Verdant and Varied

A basic evergreen wreath can easily be embellished with additional plant material. Buffy prefers to start wreaths from scratch by choosing a well-soaked floral foam ring as her base. "Plunge your greenery in buckets of water for a couple of days to really hydrate everything, and then make sure to keep displays away from heating vents to prevent your hard work from drying out quickly. A spritz of water every few days helps keep things fresh," she suggests. For this wreath, Buffy secures evenly spaced groupings of branches—silver dollar eucalyptus, olive, long-leaf pine, lemon cypress, cedar, and fir—with florists wire around the form. She chooses a rich indigo bow for an elegant finishing touch that makes a bold statement against a glossy black entry door.

"All arrangements start with good mechanics, like a floral foam cage, frog, or other materials that provide support or hold water. Refresh the water regularly, and replace any dried-out greenery or wilted plant material as needed."

P. Allen Smith's GARDEN HOME

BARBRA STREISAND My Passion for Design

ERIC MEOLA INDIA In Word & Image

Festive First Impressions

Buffy believes adding pizzazz where guests first arrive is essential, which often means the driveway. In the South, the bar for mailbox décor is sky-high. "Whether true or not, abundant mailbox displays suggest to neighbors that your whole house is equally dressed and ready for the season," she says with a wink. But, since her current home doesn't have a mailbox curbside, Buffy focuses on her foyer instead. A manzanita branch in a vase offers ample real estate for ornaments reflected in a mirror for double the drama. A floral arrangement beneath repeats the sunny palette. "I secure clusters of paperwhite stems with florists tape and tuck them between clementines in a water-filled vase. The citrus acts like a floral frog, keeping the stems where I want them." Nandina berries spill out for merry measure. As a reminder, Buffy says, "Always consider the 'filler, thriller, and spiller' formula for a balanced arrangement."

> **"Right when they bloom, cut the stamens off of flowers like amaryllis and lilies to keep the pollen from dropping and staining surfaces."**

Amaryllis by Forcing or Fooling

Often a healthy amaryllis bulb you are trying to force is slow to bloom. In that case, Buffy suggests coaxing it by putting it in a warm spot (70°F to 80°F) with bright, indirect sunlight. Rotate it regularly to develop a sturdy upright stem that supports the flowers. It's best to start forcing bulbs that do not require chilling—amaryllis, paperwhites, and crocosmia—at least 4 to 6 weeks before you want them to bloom. If patience isn't your virtue, visit the flower market and buy freshly cut amaryllis stems or turn to faux. "Quality faux flowers of today look quite real. When I use them, I mix in natural elements like fresh greenery or fruit," Buffy says. "The flowers of freshly cut amaryllis are long-lasting, and the stems make a striking display." Here, Buffy nestles a small cylindrical vase inside a larger one and arranges amaryllis stems vertically between them. She combines Interstellar and Cherry Nymph amaryllis blooms with ranunculus, juniper, and rose hips in the smaller vase.

The Contemporary Garden

Orchids

FRIEDMAN/FAIRFAX

"Some succulent leaves will break off as you work. Consider it an opportunity for propagation. Put the leaves on a windowsill inside, and plant them in a few weeks once hairy roots form."

Trimming a Tabletop Tree

Much of Buffy's year is spent decorating for others, whether it's floral installations for clients or styling for magazines. However, she prefers a more minimalist approach in her home this time of year. She likes holiday projects that can be done while connecting with friends and family, like decoupage, cooking, or painting. She says, "making gingerbread houses with the grandchildren each year creates a fun, messy memory for all of us." This tabletop arrangement was created while visiting with her sister and niece. They attached various succulents and moss varieties to cone and wreath forms from the crafts store, using U-pins and hot glue to keep everything securely in place. "You mostly can ignore these living succulent arrangements, and they'll last all season. I do mist them when the fireplace is in regular use," she says. Remove the plants from the forms after the holidays and plant them in cactus mix. In a matter of months, you will have a healthy supply to enlist in future projects. You can reuse the wreath and tree forms several times, too.

"The color of a ribbon I stumble upon or an interesting Etsy find that coordinates with my tree are often the only inspiration I need for my decorating direction."

Seasonal Showstopper

Buffy's creative talents extend in every direction, including painting. Her artwork provides a striking backdrop, reminiscent of a winter sky, for the large floral centerpiece she created for her dining room. This is where her family gathers for Christmas brunch every year, so she likes to create something extra-special. Oversize gold ornaments and fairy lights repeat the shimmer of a gilded container brimming with peonies, ranunculus, paperwhites, emerald hydrangea, parrot tulips, snapdragons, leucothoe, and mixed Christmas greenery. "I strip flower stems and evergreen branches of leaves and bundle them together with floral wire to create clusters that I tuck into the floral foam for a full look that really highlights each element," she explains. She makes sure to burn the ends of cut poinsettia stems to seal them before adding them to the mix. "This key step makes the milky sap coagulate and prevents the stems from wilting."

A Natural Noël

KATHLEEN VARNER decorates for the holidays like she means business. And as a prop stylist and floral designer, creating beautiful vignettes for photo shoots, weddings, and life's most special occasions is her business. In her holiday home, she weaves accents from Mother Nature with family heirlooms and favorite pieces collected over the years. She tucks seasonal surprises into unexpected places in addition to the waves of garland on the stairs and an elegant tree in the living room. The end result is a bit of whimsy around every corner.

"I need a sense of calm at home. I like texture, antiques, and a mix of modern and natural elements."

A Nod to Nostalgia

With two very young children, a physician-husband, and a busy career pulling her in all directions, Kathleen Varner could just hang stockings and string lights on a tree and call it "done." But instead, elements of surprise and delight abound. "I start decorating the day after Thanksgiving," she says. "I get so excited, especially having kids now. It's fun to see their wonder." Her everyday neutral style of dark and light and modern pieces mixed with antiques is an easy backdrop for a natural holiday look. "With kids' toys all about and working on so many different looks in my work, I seek calm at home. Of course, I do add extra sparkle during the holidays. Ribbon and garland...I don't think you can have enough!" She also incorporates cuttings from her Christmas tree and yard in more unexpected places, like to soften the edges of picture frames on a wall or to grace the corner of a gilded mirror.

> "Just go to the favorite spots in your home and add that extra layer."

Bright Copper and Petals

Kathleen describes her holiday look as dark and moody with an old-world feel balanced with pops of modern and glitzy. "I don't think there is such a thing as too much tinsel!" she admits. Copper ornaments and rose gold ribbon play off the velvety backsides of the magnolia leaves, rich wood tones, and animal hides and complement the varied greenery. "Simple is my motto at home because my kids are going to knock things down, so the less there is to pick up or maintain, the better!" Small decorative vignettes make an impression. "The antique urn is a piece I found for a wedding." She swaps the arrangement inside with the seasons. To keep her tree and greenery fresh, Kathleen sprays everything generously with a floral preservative spray, like Pristine, to lock in moisture. "Though if you have plans to entertain, it's best to get your greenery close to the party date. I only use faux paperwhites in my entry because I don't like the smell of fresh ones."

"Josh and I love a good cocktail by the fire this time of year, so our little bar nook gets a lot of use!"

The Holly and the Ivories

Kathleen loves to set the table. "Many of us don't have full sets of dishes or flatware, and I think mixing things up gives a table more interest and a relaxed feel anyway. I use a layered setting that complements the colors in my home, adding a touch of burnt orange for Thanksgiving and more gold for shimmer at Christmastime," she says. Both she and her husband, Josh, grew up with pianos that got played regularly. "My dad is from Nashville, so we spent Christmas with my grandmother there. Floyd Cramer was her neighbor, a well-known pianist who worked with big names in country music. So my childhood Christmas memories are set to piano music," Kathleen recalls. As a result, the baby grand piano in her living room has become essential to how they entertain this time of year. Whether it's a formal seated dinner for colleagues or an espresso martini nightcap with friends by the fire, you can bet ivory keys will be tickled.

"I love mixing and matching patterns and the old and new. As long as there is a common color woven through, you can play and have fun."

During this joyous time of year ripe for memory-making, Kathleen loves creating evocative spaces with ample nostalgia. A cheery shade of pink, vintage and contemporary pieces, and pattern play come together in a peaceful room for her daughter, Alice, that's as inviting for a child as it is for a grown-up. A whimsical display atop the dresser and greenery and wreaths hugging the windows add that touch of holiday wonder that makes Christmastime extra special at any age. Kathleen admits to getting much of her inspiration while working with so many talented designers, florists, stylists, and photographers throughout the year. Her basic formula is easy. "If you stay true to the colors in a room and stick to lots of natural accents, it always works."

Merry Remix

MINDI SHAPIRO LEVINE *kicked off her creative career in fashion before parlaying her skills into photo styling for cookbooks and magazines. Whether dressing a model for the runway, styling a retail window for the holidays, or setting an elegant table for photography for a publication, she takes an innovative approach by incorporating something unexpected or finding new uses for everyday items. Mindi launched a side business this year to feed her passion for hunting down unique pieces that she uses myriad ways. She then styles and photographs her finds to showcase their versatility and lists them for sale.*

> "You may be the only person on the block turning a faux-fur stole into your front door's holiday wreath, but you'll also be the talk of the town for your bold thinking."

Holiday Tinsel and Tie-dings

Styling for Mindi Shapiro Levine usually starts with a prop or a theme. A jumping-off point is key before diving in. "This year, I wanted to explore an idea as much as a theme. Stars, modern design, Scandinavia, and jewel tones were my foundation," she explains. And the midcentury feel of this dining room had her thinking "Madmen." So she took that and her love of fashion and ran with it. She turned an assortment of second hand-store neckties into a one-of-a-kind holiday wreath and a handsome package topper. A faux-fur stole is more glamorous than any garland of greenery on a bar cart. These details are conversation starters, which makes any party more fun. "I believe everything can be a beautiful material," she says. As another example, one minute, she sips a diet soda, and the next, she cuts the empty can with tin snips to create a frilly, reflective votive holder that takes the concept of recycling to a fanciful level.

"I imagine how I can use something familiar in a new and unexpected way."

Puttin' on the Glitz

For Mindi, the hunt never ends. "I'm always on the lookout for that perfectly imperfect piece. There are flea markets and antique malls I visit again and again knowing that they're just as likely to have sleigh bells and Santas in July as October." She also turns to what she or her clients already have. "Anything that has the right shape can be a foundation for reimagining," she explains. The shape of a full skirt is reminiscent of a Christmas tree, so she made a skirt out of magnolia leaves attached to a dressmaker's form and dressed the bodice in holiday style with a shimmery top and costume-jewelry brooches. "She would be as fantastical in a foyer to greet guests as a teenage girl's room," Mindi says. And with sequined sneakers, who needs a tree skirt? More brooches adorn ribbons and add shimmer to wrapped gifts. See another inspired tree that Mindi made from a ladder on page 168.

> **"Part of the fun is finding pieces that continuously reinforce and reimagine what lies at the heart of your concept."**

Fa La La La Folly

Even when decorating with traditional red and green, Mindi gets inventive. "I'd like to think of myself as a maximal modernist. Though I love clean lines, strong shapes, and the contemporary, I'm also passionate about warm fabrics, bold colors, and strong patterns. I see design and décor as being as much about feeling as function, but never to the exclusion of fun," she says. Decorating this outdoor space was all about fun and let Mindi strut her stuff as a maker. She bent colored wire into holiday shapes to accent gifts and grace a hanging wall tree made from birch branches and garden twine. More metalwork—soda cans, siding, and ceiling tiles—cut into Christmas tree and ornament shapes adds lots of patina. A galvanized Christmas village is tailor-made for an outdoor display behind an old metal glider, and stars cut into tin luminarias cast a warm glow at dusk. The result is a welcoming place that beckons visitors to stop and sit a spell. "Company may not be able to put it quite into words, but they'll know that everything feels familiar, connected, and right," Mindi explains.

2

Entertain

HOLIDAY MENUS

CHEERY PITCHER
CHELADAS,
PAGE 60

Merry Brunchmas

Whether you're hosting a holiday brunch or fortifying family and friends for a day of decking the halls, these festive recipes are sure to please your crowd. Most everything can be prepped ahead of time and then popped in the oven or assembled to serve.

• MENU FOR 6 •

CHEERY PITCHER CHELADAS

SMOKY PEPPER-PECAN SUGARED BACON

NUTTY GRANOLA WITH WHIPPED RICOTTA AND BERRIES

SPINACH-FETA QUICHE WITH SWEET POTATO CRUST

SPICED CRANBERRY-PECAN ROLLS

Cheery Pitcher Cheladas

SERVES **6**   ACTIVE **15 MIN.**   TOTAL **15 MIN.**

Trade the usual brunchtime bloody Mary or mimosa for this juicy spin on the Mexican Chelada, a traditional cocktail of beer mixed with citrus and spices. The addition of mango juice adds a tropical tang to this sunny eye-opener. Make a second batch for a crowd.

3 (12-oz.) bottles chilled Mexican lager

4 Tbsp. lime juice

2½ cups mango nectar

¼ tsp. cayenne pepper

1 tsp. hot sauce, plus more for serving

½ tsp. kosher salt

Tajín seasoning

Lime wedges, mango wedges, and jalapeño slices, for garnish

Hot sauce (optional)

1. Combine lager, lime juice, mango nectar, cayenne pepper, hot sauce, and salt in a large pitcher.

2. Rim 6 single old-fashioned glasses with the Tajín seasoning. Fill each glass with ice and top with beer mixture.

3. Garnish with lime wedges, mango wedges, and jalapeño slices. Serve with hot sauce to let guests adjust heat to taste.

Smoky Pepper–Pecan Sugared Bacon

SERVES **6**   ACTIVE **15 MIN.**   TOTAL **45 MIN.**

It's hard to eat just one slice of this sweet-and-savory bacon. It's delicious as a side or a Bloody Mary garnish, or try it chopped up and tossed in salads or sandwiched in a burger or grilled cheese.

2 Tbsp. coarsely chopped pecans

2 Tbsp. brown sugar

2 tsp. smoked paprika

1½ tsp. black pepper

12 thick-cut bacon slices

1. Preheat oven to 400°F. Process pecans in a food processor until finely chopped, about 20 seconds. Stir together pecans, brown sugar, smoked paprika, and pepper.

2. Place half of bacon in a single layer on a lightly greased wire rack in a foil-lined baking sheet. Repeat procedure with remaining bacon, placing on another lightly greased wire rack in a second foil-lined baking sheet. Press pecan mixture on top of bacon slices, coating well.

3. Bake in preheated oven, turning once, until browned and crisp, 22 to 25 minutes. Let stand 5 minutes.

Nutty Granola with Whipped Ricotta and Berries

SERVES **8**   ACTIVE **15 MIN.**   TOTAL **30 MIN.**

Rise and dine with these cute muffin-tin parfaits topped with festive red berries.

1¹/₂ cups old-fashioned rolled oats

³/₄ cup chopped unsalted pistachios, toasted, divided

¹/₄ tsp. ground cinnamon

¹/₈ tsp. kosher salt

4 Tbsp. honey, divided

2 Tbsp. creamy almond butter

1 large egg white

Cooking spray

2 cups ricotta

Zest of 1 orange

2 cups fresh raspberries

Chopped fresh mint, for garnish (optional)

1. Preheat oven to 325°F.

2. Combine oats, ¼ cup pistachios, cinnamon, and salt in a large bowl. Combine 3 tablespoons of the honey and the almond butter in a small microwave-safe bowl. Microwave at HIGH 20 to 30 seconds; stir until smooth. Add honey mixture and egg white to oat mixture; toss to coat. Divide oat mixture evenly among 8 muffin cups coated with cooking spray. Using a piece of parchment paper (to prevent sticking), press oat mixture into bottom and up sides of each muffin cup. Bake in preheated oven until edges are browned and crisp, about 15 minutes; cool completely in pan.

3. Carefully run an offset spatula or butter knife around edges to loosen granola cups; remove from pan.

4. Combine ricotta, remaining 1 tablespoon honey, and orange zest in a mixing bowl. Beat at medium-high speed with an electric mixer until creamy, about 2 minutes. Spoon a heaping ¼ cup of the ricotta mixture into each granola cup, and top with ¼ cup raspberries and 1 tablespoon pistachios. Garnish with mint, if desired.

Spinach–Feta Quiche with Sweet Potato Crust

SERVES **6**   ACTIVE **25 MIN.**   TOTAL **1 HOUR, 10 MIN.**

A crust made from thinly sliced rounds of sweet potato makes this quiche gluten-free. Choose potatoes of a similar diameter to create uniform slices for the crust. A mandoline or food processor fitted with the slicing blade makes slicing quick and precise, but a sharp chef's knife works, too.

Cooking spray

2 medium sweet potatoes, peeled and cut into 1/8-inch-thick slices

1 tsp. canola oil

1/2 cup sliced red onion

1 (5-oz.) bag fresh baby spinach

1/2 cup whole milk

1/4 tsp. kosher salt

1/4 tsp. black pepper

1/4 tsp. crushed red pepper

1/4 tsp. grated nutmeg

6 large eggs

2 oz. Parmigiano-Reggiano cheese, grated (about 1/2 cup)

1 1/2 oz. feta cheese, crumbled (about 1/3 cup)

1. Preheat oven to 350°F.

2. Coat a 9-inch pie plate with cooking spray. Layer sweet potatoes in slightly overlapping concentric circles on bottom and up sides of plate, cutting slices in half to fit (rounded side up) around the sides. Coat potatoes with cooking spray. Bake until potatoes are slightly tender, about 20 minutes. Place pan on a wire rack. Increase oven temperature to 375°F.

3. Heat a large nonstick skillet over medium. Add oil and onion; sauté 3 minutes. Add spinach; sauté 3 minutes. Remove from heat; cool.

4. Combine milk, salt, black pepper, red pepper, nutmeg, eggs, and Parmigiano-Reggiano cheese in a medium bowl; stir with a whisk. Arrange spinach mixture in crust; pour egg mixture over spinach. Sprinkle with feta. Bake in preheated oven until egg mixture is set, about 35 minutes. Let stand 5 minutes; cut into 6 wedges.

CHEERY
PITCHER
CHELADAS,
PAGE 60

NUTTY GRANOLA WITH
WHIPPED RICOTTA
AND BERRIES,
PAGE 63

SPINACH-FETA QUICHE
WITH SWEET POTATO
CRUST, PAGE 64

SMOKY
PEPPER-PECAN
SUGARED BACON,
PAGE 60

Spiced Cranberry-Pecan Rolls

MAKES **12 ROLLS** ACTIVE **20 MIN.**
TOTAL **1 HOUR, 20 MIN.**

*No holiday morning is complete without something hot
from the oven and something sweet. This ticks both
boxes. The dough is made with a packaged mix and
rises in just 30 minutes.*

1 cup chopped pecans

1 cup dried cranberries

1 (16-oz.) pkg. hot
roll mix

½ cup butter, softened

1 cup firmly packed light
brown sugar

2 tsp. ground pumpkin
pie spice

1 cup powdered sugar

2 Tbsp. milk

1 tsp. vanilla extract

1. Preheat oven to 350°F. Bake pecans in a single layer in
a shallow pan 5 to 7 minutes or until toasted and fragrant,
stirring halfway through.

2. Soak dried cranberries in a bowl with hot water to cover for
15 minutes. Drain and set aside.

3. Prepare hot roll dough as directed on back of package;
let dough stand 5 minutes. Roll dough into a 15- x 10-inch
rectangle; spread with softened butter. Stir together brown
sugar and pumpkin pie spice; sprinkle over butter. Sprinkle
chopped pecans over brown sugar mixture. Sprinkle
cranberries over pecans. Roll up dough tightly, starting at one
long end; cut into 12 slices. Place rolls, cut sides down, in a
lightly greased 12-inch cast-iron skillet or 13- x 9-inch pan.
Cover loosely with plastic wrap and a kitchen towel; let rise
in a warm place (85°F), free from drafts, until doubled in bulk,
about 30 minutes.

4. Preheat oven to 375°F. Uncover rolls. Bake in preheated oven
until center rolls are golden brown and done, 20 to 25 minutes.

5. Let cool in pan on a wire rack 10 minutes. Stir together
powdered sugar, milk, and vanilla; drizzle over rolls.

BLUSHING
PALOMA PUNCH,
PAGE 72

Ho Ho Hoedown

Festive should be fun, but it doesn't have to be fancy. Dust off your cowboy boots, snow boots, or garden boots and ring in the season with this relaxed affair bursting with South by Southwest flavor and accented with warm, rustic holiday touches.

· MENU FOR 10 ·

BLUSHING PALOMA PUNCH
JALAPEÑO POPPER DIP
SMOKY POTATO SKIN BITES
BOURBON AND CHERRY GLAZED BRISKET
APPLE-CABBAGE SLAW
PECAN-CORN MUFFINS
CARAMEL THUMBPRINT TARTLETS

Blushing Paloma Punch

SERVES **16**   ACTIVE **5 MIN.**   TOTAL **5 MIN.**

Paloma means "dove" in Spanish. The cocktail is a refreshing mix of tequila (or a nonalcoholic substitute; see box at right), grapefruit soda, and lime juice. This punchbowl rendition does wonders for holiday spirits with its grapefruit trio—juice, soda, and liqueur—and the holiday blush it gets from the addition of cranberry juice.

1 (52-oz.) bottle refrigerated grapefruit juice

1 (52-oz.) bottle refrigerated limeade

3 (12-oz.) bottles grapefruit soda

4½ cups (36 oz.) tequila

1½ cups (12 oz.) pamplemousse liqueur

¾ cup cranberry juice

½ cup agave nectar

2 limes, sliced

2 red grapefruits, sliced

Frozen cranberries and fresh jalapeño slices, for garnish (optional)

Stir together grapefruit juice, limeade, grapefruit soda, tequila, pamplemousse liqueur, cranberry juice, and agave nectar in a punch bowl. Add citrus slices. Garnish with cranberries and jalapeño slices, if desired.

Agave Spirits

Many types of spirits are made from the fermentation and distillation of crushed agave plants. Agaves are roasted in ovens for tequila and over wood coals for mezcal. Other agave spirits include raicilla, bacanora, sotol, and the bubbly beer-like pulque, which are less readily available in the United States. Types of nonalcoholic "tequilas" are available now, such as those produced by Lyre, Ritual, Free Spirits, and Mockingbird brands.

Jalapeño Popper Dip

SERVES **12**   ACTIVE **15 MIN.**   TOTAL **30 MIN.**

The yumminess of jalapeño poppers morphs into a creamy, crowd-pleasing dip that's perfect for scooping with chips or crudités. If you want to take your hors d'oeuvres game to new heights, you could spoon the dip inside hollowed-out jalapeño peppers and wrap them in bacon for grilling.

1 (1-lb.) pkg. center-cut bacon, cooked and crumbled, divided

2 (8-oz.) pkg. cream cheese, softened

1 cup mayonnaise

1 cup sour cream

2 tsp. taco seasoning

6 fresh jalapeño chiles (5 seeded and minced, 1 thinly sliced)

1 cup sliced scallions, divided

1 (1-lb.) pkg. shredded Mexican cheese blend, divided

¼ cup chopped fresh cilantro

Tortilla chips, for serving

Crudités, for serving

1. Preheat oven to 350°F. Set aside ¼ cup crumbled bacon.

2. Stir together remaining bacon, the cream cheese, mayonnaise, sour cream, taco seasoning, minced jalapeños, and ¾ cup sliced scallions in a mixing bowl.

3. Set aside ½ cup shredded cheese. Fold remaining shredded cheese into cream cheese mixture to incorporate. Transfer to an ovenproof baking dish. Top with reserved bacon, sliced jalapeño, and remaining scallions. Bake in preheated oven until bubbly, 20 to 30 minutes.

4. Sprinkle with cilantro. Serve with tortilla chips and crudités.

Smoky Potato Skin Bites

MAKES **20**   ACTIVE **30 MIN.**   TOTAL **1 HOUR, 45 MIN.**

This hearty nibble travels well. To take these to a party, prepare the recipe through Step 3, and place the potato skins in a container. Then, complete Step 4 just before serving.

1 to 1½ lb. baby Dutch yellow potatoes (about 20 [2-inch] potatoes)

1 Tbsp. olive oil

4 oz. smoked cheddar or Gouda cheese, shredded (about 1 cup)

6 mesquite-smoked bacon slices, cooked and crumbled

½ cup sour cream

2 Tbsp. chopped fresh thyme or chives

Pickled jalapeño slices, for garnish (optional)

1. Preheat oven to 425°F. Scrub potatoes, and pat dry thoroughly. Place potatoes in a large bowl, and drizzle with olive oil; toss to coat. Arrange potatoes in a single layer on a baking sheet lined with parchment paper. Bake in preheated oven until tender, 17 to 20 minutes. Cool potatoes completely on baking sheet, about 30 minutes.

2. Slice potatoes in half lengthwise, and scoop out potato flesh, leaving ⅛-inch-thick shells. Reserve potato flesh for another use (such as mashed potatoes).

3. Increase oven temperature to 450°F. Place potato skins, hollowed side down, on baking sheet lined with parchment paper. Bake 10 minutes; flip potatoes over, and bake until crispy, 8 to 10 minutes longer.

4. Fill potato skins evenly with cheese, and top with bacon crumbles. Bake until cheese melts, 1 to 2 minutes. Top each potato skin with a dollop of sour cream, and sprinkle evenly with chopped fresh thyme. Garnish with pickled jalapeño slices, if desired.

NOTE: *For topping potato skins with neat dollops of sour cream, use a zip-top plastic bag with one corner snipped off.*

APPLE-CABBAGE
SLAW,
PAGE 76

SMOKY POTATO
SKIN BITES,
PAGE 73

PECAN-CORN
MUFFINS,
PAGE 77

JALAPEÑO POPPER DIP, PAGE 73

BOURBON AND CHERRY GLAZED BRISKET, PAGE 76

Bourbon and Cherry Glazed Brisket

SERVES **12** ACTIVE **40 MIN.** TOTAL **8 HOURS**

Offer warm tortillas for those who prefer to eat taco-style.

1 (6-lb.) beef brisket

2 Tbsp. kosher salt, divided

2 tsp. black pepper, divided

Cooking spray

1 large yellow onion, vertically sliced (about 4 cups)

2 tsp. chipotle chile powder

2 cups beef broth

1 cup bourbon

1 Tbsp. liquid smoke

2 Tbsp. plus 2 tsp. balsamic vinegar, divided

8 bay leaves

1 (14.1-oz) jar Luxardo maraschino cherries

24 large white bread slices (1/2-inch-thick)

1 small white onion, thinly sliced (1 cup)

Sliced white bread, dill pickle chips, and pickled jalapeño slices, for serving

Fresh rosemary sprigs, for garnish (optional)

1. Rub brisket with 4 teaspoons of the salt and 1 teaspoon of the black pepper. Coat a large, heavy skillet with cooking spray, and place over medium-high. Brown brisket on all sides, about 10 minutes. Transfer beef to an 8-quart slow cooker. Add onion, remaining salt and black pepper, and the chipotle chile powder to skillet; cook until tender, about 5 minutes. Add beef broth, bourbon, liquid smoke, and 2 tablespoons of the balsamic vinegar to skillet, stirring to loosen browned bits from bottom. Bring to a boil; cook 4 minutes. Pour mixture over beef; add bay leaves and strained cherries from the jar, reserving syrup.

2. Cover and cook on LOW until tender, but not falling apart, 7 to 7½ hours. Discard bay leaves. Thinly slice across the grain.

3. Strain liquid into a medium saucepan, discarding solids. Add the cherry syrup to liquid. Boil over medium-high, and then simmer until reduced by half, about 20 minutes. Stir in remaining 2 teaspoons balsamic vinegar; simmer until slightly thickened, about 5 minutes. Serve brisket with sauce, sliced white bread, dill pickle chips, and pickled jalapeño slices. Garnish with rosemary, if desired.

Apple-Cabbage Slaw

SERVES **10** ACTIVE **10 MIN.** TOTAL **10 MIN.**

The packaged convenience of dried fruit and nut mix delivers color, flavor, and crunch to this simple slaw. Other crisp, sweet-tart apple varieties that would work well here include Sweet Tango, Jazz, or Honeycrisp.

1/2 cup canola oil

1/4 cup apple cider vinegar

3 Tbsp. honey

3/4 tsp. kosher salt

1/4 tsp. black pepper

2 (10-oz.) pkg. finely shredded cabbage

1 1/2 cups dried fruit and nut mix

3 Pink Lady apples, cored and finely chopped

4 scallions, minced

Whisk together oil, vinegar, honey, salt, and pepper in a large bowl; add cabbage, fruit and nut mix, apples, and scallions. Toss well. Cover and chill until ready to serve.

Pecan-Corn Muffins

MAKES **2 DOZEN**   ACTIVE **15 MIN.**
TOTAL **45 MIN., INCLUDING BUTTER**

Whip up the Rosemary-Maple Butter to serve with these savory muffins. Depending on your crowd, you can double this recipe. Leftover muffins freeze beautifully.

2 cups yellow self-rising cornmeal mix

1 Tbsp. granulated sugar

1/2 tsp. cayenne pepper

2 cups buttermilk

1 large egg

1 cup finely chopped toasted pecans

Cooking spray

Rosemary-Maple Butter (recipe follows)

1. Preheat oven to 425°F.

2. Stir together cornmeal mix, sugar, and cayenne pepper in a medium bowl. Whisk together buttermilk and egg; add to cornmeal mixture, stirring just until moistened. Stir in pecans.

3. Spoon 1 tablespoon of batter into each cup of two 12-cup nonstick mini muffin pans coated with cooking spray. Bake in preheated oven until a toothpick in center of a muffin comes out clean, 10 to 12 minutes. Place pans on a wire rack to cool 5 minutes. Remove muffins to rack to cool slightly. Serve warm with Rosemary-Maple Butter.

Rosemary-Maple Butter

Combine ¼ cup dark maple syrup, ½ cup softened unsalted butter, and 2 tablespoons chopped fresh rosemary until blended. Season with salt to taste. Transfer to a sheet of parchment paper and roll into a log. Secure ends. Store in refrigerator up to 1 month.

Caramel Thumbprint Tartlets

MAKES **3 DOZEN**   ACTIVE **30 MIN.**
TOTAL **4 HOURS, 30 MIN., INCLUDING PASTRY**

Add a festive touch! Before serving, sprinkle the tarts with finely chopped chocolate, crystallized ginger, toffee, sea salt, or toasted pecans.

1 cup granulated sugar, divided

1/4 cup cold butter, sliced

3 Tbsp. all-purpose flour

2 large egg yolks

1 cup milk

Cream Cheese Pastry Shells (recipe follows)

Sweetened whipped cream

1. Cook ½ cup of the sugar in a medium-size heavy skillet over medium, stirring constantly, until sugar melts and turns golden brown, 6 to 8 minutes. Stir in butter until melted.

2. Whisk together flour, egg yolks, milk, and remaining ½ cup sugar in a heavy saucepan; bring just to a simmer over low, whisking constantly. Add sugar mixture to flour mixture, and cook until thickened, whisking constantly, 1 to 2 minutes. Cover and chill 4 hours.

3. Meanwhile, prepare Cream Cheese Pastry Shells. Spoon caramel mixture into pastry shells, and top with sweetened whipped cream.

Cream Cheese Pastry Shells

1/2 cup butter, softened

1/2 (8-oz.) pkg. cream cheese, softened

1 1/4 cups all-purpose flour

1. Beat butter and cream cheese at medium speed with a heavy-duty electric stand mixer until creamy. Gradually add flour to butter mixture, beating at low speed just until blended. Shape dough into 36 (¾-inch) balls, and place on a baking sheet; cover and chill 1 hour.

2. Preheat oven to 400°F. Place dough balls in cups of lightly greased miniature muffin pans; press dough to top of cups, forming shells.

3. Bake in preheated oven until golden, 10 to 12 minutes. Remove from pans to wire racks, and cool completely. Makes 36 shells.

TIP: *Baked pastry shells may be made up to 1 month ahead and frozen in an airtight container. Thaw at room temperature before filling.*

MAKE-AHEAD
YEAST ROLLS,
PAGE 83

MESCLUN, PEAR, AND
GOAT CHEESE SALAD,
PAGE 84

Homecoming Feast

The Christmas season is about coming home to the people we love and the places we cherish. So often, guests arrive after harried travel days or busy workdays. Yet, once they step across the threshold to familiar faces, the aromas of woodsmoke and pine, and the delicious scents wafting from the kitchen, stress morphs into good spirits as if by magic. And soon the feasting begins!

· MENU FOR 8 ·

RUBY NEGRONI

BACON-BOURBON FIG BITES

MAKE-AHEAD YEAST ROLLS

SWEET POTATO SOUP WITH FRIED SAGE LEAVES

MESCLUN, PEAR, AND GOAT CHEESE SALAD

CRUSTY SPINACH CASSEROLE

WILD RICE WITH BACON AND FENNEL

PORK ROAST WITH VIDALIA-PEPITA RELISH

CHOCOLATE-TOFFEE-GINGERBREAD CAKE

Ruby Negroni

SERVES **12**   ACTIVE **10 MIN.**   TOTAL **10 MIN.**

This twist on the classic Negroni features ruby red pomegranate juice for a festive drink to ring in any holiday gathering. Make it a mocktail by substituting nonalcoholic gin for the regular gin and Giffard Aperitif Syrup for the bitter Campari.

4 cups (32 oz.) pomegranate juice

2 cups (16 oz.) gin

2 cups (16 oz.) Campari

2 cups (16 oz.) sweet vermouth

Crushed ice

3 cups (24 oz.) club soda

Fresh orange slices, for garnish

1. Stir together pomegranate juice, gin, Campari, and vermouth in a pitcher. Cover and chill.

2. Fill 12 double old-fashioned glasses with crushed ice. Divide juice mixture evenly among glasses. Top each serving with ¼ cup club soda, and stir gently. Garnish with orange slices. Serve immediately.

Bacon-Bourbon Fig Bites

MAKES **2 DOZEN**   ACTIVE **30 MIN.**   TOTAL **45 MIN.**

The size of the figs will determine the amount of cheese you'll need for these bite-size delights.

12 dried Calimyrna figs

¼ cup bourbon

1 (2- to 4-oz.) wedge Gorgonzola cheese, cut into 24 pieces

24 toasted pecan halves

12 fully cooked bacon slices, cut in half crosswise

Wooden picks

1. Preheat oven to 350°F.

2. Combine figs, bourbon, and 1½ cups water in a medium saucepan. Cover and cook over low until figs are plump and softened, 15 to 20 minutes. Remove from heat; cool slightly (about 15 minutes). Drain figs; gently pat dry with paper towels.

3. Cut figs in half lengthwise. Place 1 cheese piece and 1 pecan half on cut side of each fig half. Wrap 1 bacon piece around each fig, and secure with a wooden pick. Place on a wire rack in a 15- x 10-inch jelly-roll pan.

4. Bake in preheated oven until bacon is crisp and browned, 6 to 8 minutes.

Make-Ahead Yeast Rolls

MAKES **16**   ACTIVE **15 MIN.**

TOTAL **10 HOURS, 45 MIN., INCLUDING PROOFING,
RISING, AND CHILLING**

*Warm and comforting, these pillowy rolls are quick to
disappear. Serve with sweet cream butter or Rosemary-
Maple Butter (page 77).*

2 (¼-oz.) envelopes
active dry yeast

4½ to 5 cups all-purpose
flour, divided

3 large eggs

½ cup shortening,
melted

½ cup granulated sugar

2 tsp. kosher salt

1. Stir together yeast and ¼ cup warm water (100°F to 110°F) in
a small bowl; let stand 5 minutes or until bubbly.

2. Stir together yeast mixture, 1 cup warm water (100°F to
110°F), 2 cups flour, the eggs, shortening, sugar, and salt in a
large bowl. Beat with a wooden spoon 2 minutes. Gradually
stir in enough remaining flour to make a soft dough.

3. Cover and let rise in a warm place (80°F to 85°F), free from
drafts, 1 hour.

4. Deflate dough, cover, and chill at least 8 hours.

5. Deflate dough and turn out onto a floured surface. Knead
4 turns. Shape dough into 16 (2-inch) balls. Divide dough balls
between 2 lightly greased 9-inch square pans. Cover and
let rise in a warm place (80°F to 85°F), free from drafts, until
doubled in bulk, about 1½ hours.

6.. Preheat oven to 375°F. Bake in preheated oven until golden,
about 12 minutes.

Sweet Potato Soup with Fried Sage Leaves

MAKES **8 CUPS** ACTIVE **35 MIN.**

TOTAL **1 HOUR, 5 MIN., INCLUDING FRIED SAGE**

Make the soup through Step 2 the day before. Reheat and stir in the lime juice before serving.

2 Tbsp. butter

1 medium-size onion, chopped

2 garlic cloves, minced

5½ cups reduced-sodium fat-free chicken broth

2 lb. sweet potatoes (2 large), peeled and chopped

1 cup apple cider

1 tsp. minced canned chipotle pepper in adobo sauce

1 tsp. kosher salt

2 Tbsp. plus 2 tsp. fresh lime juice, divided

½ cup sour cream

Fried Sage Leaves (recipe follows)

Crushed red pepper, for garnish (optional)

1. Melt butter in a large saucepan over medium-high; add onion, and sauté 5 to 7 minutes or until tender. Add garlic; sauté 1 minute. Stir in broth, potatoes, chipotle pepper, and salt. Bring to a boil; reduce heat to medium-low, and simmer 20 minutes or until potatoes are tender.

2. Process mixture with a handheld blender until smooth. (Or, cool mixture 10 minutes, and process, in batches, in a blender until smooth. Return to saucepan, and proceed with Step 3.)

3. Cook potato mixture over low, stirring occasionally, 5 minutes or until thoroughly heated. Stir in 2 tablespoons lime juice. Whisk together sour cream and remaining 2 teaspoons lime juice in a small bowl. Ladle soup into bowls, and drizzle each serving with sour cream mixture. Top with Fried Sage Leaves and crushed red pepper, if desired.

Fried Sage Leaves

Heat ¼ cup olive oil in a small skillet over medium-high until it shimmers. Fry 30 small sage leaves in batches, 6 to 8 leaves at a time, about 3 seconds. Remove with a slotted spoon to paper towels. Sprinkle with kosher salt. Makes about 1 cup.

Mesclun, Pear, and Goat Cheese Salad

SERVES **8** ACTIVE **15 MIN.** TOTAL **15 MIN.**

This colorful salad is full of bright flavor thanks to the ample dose of pear preserves incorporated into a classic vinaigrette. Substitute toasted pecans for the walnuts if you wish.

¼ cup plus 2 Tbsp. pear preserves, divided

½ cup champagne vinegar

1 shallot, sliced

2 tsp. Dijon mustard

½ tsp. kosher salt

¼ tsp. black pepper

½ cup olive oil

8 cups loosely packed mesclun mix

2 Bartlett pears, cut into 6 wedges each

4 oz. goat cheese, crumbled

¼ cup chopped toasted walnuts

1. Process ¼ cup preserves, the vinegar, shallot, mustard, salt, and pepper in a food processor until smooth, 30 seconds to 1 minute. With processor running, pour oil through food chute in a slow, steady stream, processing until smooth. Transfer to a 2-cup measuring cup or small bowl, and stir in remaining 2 tablespoons pear preserves.

2. Place mesclun mix in a large serving bowl. Top with pears, goat cheese, and walnuts. Drizzle with vinaigrette.

RUBY NEGRONI,
PAGE 82

BACON-BOURBON
FIG BITES, PAGE 82

MAKE-AHEAD
YEAST ROLLS,
PAGE 83

PORK ROAST
WITH
VIDALIA-PEPITA
RELISH,
PAGE 89

CRUSTY
SPINACH
CASSEROLE,
PAGE 88

WILD RICE
WITH BACON
AND FENNEL,
PAGE 89

Crusty Spinach Casserole

SERVES **8 TO 10**   ACTIVE **20 MIN.**   TOTAL **50 MIN.**

With its crunchy herbed topping, this quick, cheesy side dish can be ready to bake in about the same time it takes for the oven to preheat. Place the shoestring potatoes in a zipped freezer bag and roll over it with a rolling pin a time or two for the perfect texture.

2 Tbsp. butter

1 medium-size onion, diced

2 garlic cloves, minced

4 (10-oz.) pkg. frozen chopped spinach, thawed

1/2 (7.5-oz.) container garlic and herb cream cheese, softened

2 Tbsp. all-purpose flour

2 large eggs

1/2 tsp. kosher salt

1/4 tsp. black pepper

1 cup milk

1 (8-oz.) pkg. shredded Italian blend cheese

1 (9-oz.) can shoestring potatoes, lightly crushed

3 Tbsp. butter, melted

3 Tbsp. chopped fresh chives

1. Preheat oven to 350°F. Melt 2 tablespoons butter in a large nonstick skillet over medium. Add onion and garlic, and cook, stirring occasionally, 8 minutes or until tender.

2. Meanwhile, drain spinach well, pressing between paper towels to remove excess moisture.

3. Combine cream cheese and flour in a large bowl until smooth. Whisk in eggs, salt, and pepper. Gradually whisk in milk until blended. Add onion mixture, spinach, and cheese, stirring to blend. Spoon into a lightly greased 11- x 7-inch baking dish.

4. Combine shoestring potatoes, melted butter, and chives in a small bowl; toss well, and sprinkle over casserole.

5. Bake, uncovered, in preheated oven until thoroughly heated and topping is browned, 30 to 35 minutes.

Upper Crusts

A good casserole is the little black dress of Southern comfort foods, but it's often the sweet and savory toppings that make a casserole sing. Here are three all-star options we love.

Cornflakes
A hefty sprinkling of the crushed flakes on top of a savory casserole delivers a just-right, so-light crunch. Try it on top of the Jalapeño Popper Dip (page 73).

Ritz Crackers
Combine the crumbs of this buttery cracker with Parmesan cheese and layered on top of your favorite casserole: oyster dressing, poppy seed chicken, or the Crusty Spinach Casserole (at left).

Canned French Fried Onions
Crispy, crunchy, and sweet, fried onions turn any green bean casserole into a side-dish hero. Use them in place of the bacon-flavored breadcrumbs (page 125) in a pinch.

Wild Rice with Bacon and Fennel

SERVES **8**   ACTIVE **40 MIN.**   TOTAL **1 HOUR, 5 MIN.**

Use wild rice, not a blend, for the best texture.

1¹/₃ cups uncooked wild rice

4 bacon slices

1 large fennel bulb, thinly sliced

1 large onion, cut into thin wedges

2 garlic cloves, minced

¹/₂ cup reduced-sodium fat-free chicken broth

¹/₃ cup golden raisins

¹/₄ tsp. kosher salt

¹/₈ tsp. black pepper

¹/₄ cup chopped fresh fennel fronds or flat-leaf parsley

1 Tbsp. white wine vinegar

¹/₂ cup chopped toasted walnuts

1. Cook wild rice according to package directions; drain.

2. Meanwhile, cook bacon in a large nonstick skillet over medium-high until crisp, 7 to 8 minutes; drain on paper towels, reserving 1 tablespoon drippings in skillet. Chop bacon.

3. Sauté fennel bulb and onion in hot drippings over medium-high 5 minutes or until softened. Add garlic; sauté 1 minute. Add broth, raisins, salt, and pepper; bring to a boil. Reduce heat to medium-low; cover and simmer 8 minutes or until tender. Stir in rice and bacon; cook, stirring often, 3 minutes.

4. Transfer to a large serving bowl. Stir in fennel fronds and vinegar. Stir in walnuts just before serving.

Pork Roast with Vidalia-Pepita Relish

SERVES **8**   ACTIVE **20 MIN.**   TOTAL **1 HOUR, 50 MIN.**

Be sure to ask your butcher to cut out the chine bone and to french the rib rack for easy carving and an elegant presentation.

1¹/₄ tsp. kosher salt, divided

¹/₂ tsp. plus ¹/₈ tsp. black pepper, divided

1 (5-lb.) 8-rib bone-in pork loin roast, chine bone removed

1 Tbsp. minced fresh rosemary

4 tsp. minced fresh thyme, divided

3 large Vidalia onions (about 2 lb.), cut into ¹/₂-inch-thick rings)

2 Tbsp. olive oil

1 tsp. white wine vinegar

1 tsp. light brown sugar

¹/₄ cup toasted pumpkin seeds (pepitas)

1. Preheat oven to 450°F. Sprinkle 1 teaspoon salt and ¹/₂ teaspoon pepper over pork; rub rosemary and 1 tablespoon thyme over pork. Place pork in a lightly greased roasting pan.

2. Toss together onions, olive oil, and remaining ¹/₄ teaspoon salt and ¹/₈ teaspoon pepper until coated. Arrange onions around pork.

3. Bake in preheated oven 30 minutes; reduce oven temperature to 375°F. Bake 50 more minutes or until a meat thermometer inserted into thickest portion registers 145°F, stirring onions once. Transfer pork to a cutting board; cover loosely with aluminum foil, and let stand 10 minutes before slicing.

4. Meanwhile, coarsely chop onions; transfer to a bowl. Add vinegar, brown sugar, and remaining 1 teaspoon thyme. Stir in pumpkin seeds before serving. Serve pork with relish.

Chocolate-Toffee-Gingerbread Cake

SERVES **10 TO 12**   ACTIVE **1 HOUR, 15 MIN.**
TOTAL **5 HOURS, 15 MIN., INCLUDING WHIPPED CREAM AND GANACHE**

Surprisingly, the addition of hot water at the end of the recipe is what makes this an exceptionally moist cake.

Ginger Whipped Cream (recipe follows)

1½ cups semisweet chocolate morsels

1 (16-oz.) pkg. light brown sugar

½ cup butter, softened

3 large eggs

2 cups all-purpose flour

¾ tsp. ground ginger

¾ tsp. ground cinnamon

½ tsp. kosher salt

½ tsp. ground allspice

¼ tsp. ground nutmeg

1 (8-oz.) container sour cream

½ cup molasses

1 tsp. baking soda

2 tsp. vanilla extract

Silky Ganache (recipe page 92)

1 cup toffee bits

Spiced Sorghum Cookies (recipe page 92), fresh cranberries, fresh rosemary, cinnamon sticks, and star anise, for garnish

1. Preheat oven to 350°F. Prepare Ginger Whipped Cream as directed in Step 1 (through chilling).

2. Microwave chocolate morsels in a microwave-safe bowl at HIGH 1 to 1½ minutes or until melted and smooth, stirring at 30-second intervals.

3. Beat brown sugar and butter with an electric mixer on medium speed until well blended, about 5 minutes. Add eggs, 1 at a time, beating just until blended after each addition. Add melted chocolate, beating just until blended.

4. Sift together flour, ginger, cinnamon, salt, allspice, and nutmeg in a separate bowl. Gradually add to chocolate mixture alternately with sour cream, beginning and ending with flour mixture. Beat at low speed just until blended after each addition. Stir together 1 cup hot water, the molasses, and baking soda. (Mixture will foam.) Gradually stir molasses mixture and vanilla into chocolate mixture just until blended. Spoon batter into 3 greased and floured 8-inch round cake pans.

5. Bake in preheated oven until a wooden pick inserted in center comes out clean, 25 to 30 minutes. Cool in pans on wire racks 10 minutes; remove from pans to wire racks, and cool completely (about 1 hour).

6. Meanwhile, prepare Silky Ganache. Place 1 cake layer on a cake stand or serving plate. Spread with half of ganache; sprinkle with ½ cup toffee bits. Top with second cake layer; spread with remaining ganache, and sprinkle with remaining ½ cup toffee bits. Top with remaining cake layer. Cover and chill 2 to 8 hours.

7. Finish preparing Ginger Whipped Cream as directed in Step 2. Spread top and sides of cake with whipped cream just before serving. Arrange Sorghum Cookies, cranberries, rosemary, cinnamon sticks, and star anise on top of cake.

Ginger Whipped Cream

2 cups heavy cream

5 (⅛-inch-thick) slices peeled fresh ginger

6 Tbsp. powdered sugar

1. Cook cream and ginger in a heavy nonaluminum saucepan over medium-high, stirring often, just until bubbles appear, 3 to 5 minutes (do not boil). Remove from heat, and let cool completely, about 20 minutes. Chill 4 to 12 hours. (Cream needs to be ice-cold before beating.)

2. Pour cream mixture through a fine wire-mesh strainer into a bowl, discarding ginger. Beat with an electric mixer on medium-high speed 1 minute or until foamy; increase speed to high, and gradually add powdered sugar, beating just until stiff peaks form, 2 to 3 minutes. (Do not overbeat or cream will become grainy.) Use immediately. Makes 4 cups.

Silky Ganache

1 (12-oz.) pkg. semisweet chocolate morsels

¹⁄₄ tsp. kosher salt

1 (14-oz.) can sweetened condensed milk

2 Tbsp. butter

1 tsp. vanilla extract

2 Tbsp. heavy cream

1. Pour water to depth of 1 inch into bottom of a double boiler over medium-high, and bring to a boil. Reduce heat to medium-low, and simmer; place chocolate and salt in top of double boiler over simmering water. Cook, stirring constantly, until melted, 2 to 3 minutes.

2. Add sweetened condensed milk; cook, stirring constantly, 1 to 2 minutes or until blended and smooth. Remove from heat; add butter and vanilla, and stir 4 to 5 minutes or until smooth.

3. Let cool to room temperature (about 45 minutes). Transfer to a bowl. Gradually add cream to chocolate mixture, and beat with an electric mixer on high speed until smooth and the consistency of a thick buttercream frosting, 2 to 3 minutes. Use immediately. Makes 2¾ cups.

Spiced Sorghum Cookies

MAKES **ABOUT 7 DOZEN**   ACTIVE **1 HOUR, 45 MIN.**
TOTAL **3 HOURS, INCLUDING ICING**

Perfect for gift giving or tucking inside a stocking, these beautiful crisp cookies are flavored with sorghum syrup and a blend of gingerbread spices.

¹⁄₂ cup butter, softened

¹⁄₄ cup granulated sugar

¹⁄₄ cup firmly packed dark brown sugar

2 tsp. orange zest

1 large egg

1 tsp. baking soda

¹⁄₂ cup sorghum syrup

3 cups all-purpose flour

4 tsp. ground pumpkin pie spice

¹⁄₄ tsp. kosher salt

Parchment paper

Royal Icing (recipe follows) (optional)

White sparkling sugar, nonpareils, and sugar pearls (optional)

1. Beat butter and sugars in the bowl of a heavy-duty electric stand mixer on medium speed until fluffy. Add orange zest and egg, beating until smooth.

2. Stir together 3 tablespoons hot water and the baking soda in a small bowl until baking soda is dissolved. Stir in sorghum syrup.

3. Stir together flour, pie spice, and salt; add to butter mixture alternately with sorghum syrup mixture, beginning and ending with flour mixture.

4. Divide dough into 2 equal portions; flatten each into a disk. Cover and chill at least 1 hour or until firm.

5. Preheat oven to 325°F. Place 1 portion of dough on a lightly floured surface, and roll to ¼-inch thickness. Cut with desired shaped cutters. Place cookies 1 inch apart on parchment paper-lined baking sheets. Repeat procedure with remaining dough disk. (Once cookies are cut and placed on baking sheets, place in freezer. Freezing them about 10 minutes allows them to better hold their shape during baking.)

6. Bake in preheated oven until cookies are puffed and slightly darker around the edges, 13 to 15 minutes. Cool on pans 1 minute; transfer to wire racks, and cool completely (about 30 minutes).

7. If using, spoon Royal Icing into a zip-top plastic freezer bag. Snip 1 corner of bag to make a small hole. Pipe icing in decorative designs on each cookie. Sprinkle with white sparkling sugar, and decorate with nonpareils and sugar pearls. Let icing harden at least 1 hour.

Royal Icing

1 (16-oz.) pkg. powdered sugar

3 Tbsp. meringue powder

1. Beat powdered sugar, meringue powder, and ½ cup warm water with an electric mixer on low speed until blended. Beat at high speed 4 minutes or until glossy and stiff peaks form, adding a few drops of additional warm water, if necessary, for desired consistency. Makes 3 cups.

CHAMPAGNE WITH
SPARKLING CRANBERRIES,
PAGE 96

"App-y" New Year!

Throwing this elegant cocktail party to ring in 2024 is as simple as a visit to the grocery store. A handful of prepared convenience items and an hour or two spent assembling this mix of hot and cold appetizers with your friends or family is all it takes. So queue up your favorite playlist and have some fun in the kitchen before raising a glass to celebrate the promise for the year ahead.

• MENU FOR 8 •

CHAMPAGNE COCKTAIL WITH SPARKLING CRANBERRIES

PIG PINWHEELS

SHRIMP COCKTAIL WITH FIVE-INGREDIENT COCKTAIL SAUCE

FETA FONDUE

RELISH TRAY SKEWERS

APRICOT-GORGONZOLA BITES

PROSCIUTTO-ASPARAGUS WRAPS

SOUTHERN-STYLE AFFOGATO

Champagne Cocktail with Sparkling Cranberries

MAKES **1**   ACTIVE **20 MIN.**
TOTAL **8 HOURS, 20 MIN., INCLUDING SPARKLING CRANBERRIES**

This effervescent cocktail from the mid-1800s is tailor-made for toasting. If a cocktail could show off, this made-to-order one is it. It's super simple to make yet so elegant to sip. Substitute sparkling pear juice for a festive mocktail instead.

1 sugar cube

3 to 5 dashes Angostura bitters

Champagne or sparkling white wine, chilled

Lemon peel strip

Sparkling Cranberries (recipe follows)

1. Drop sugar cube in bottom of a champagne flute. Add bitters to soak sugar cube. Top with Champagne. Add lemon peel strip.

2. Skewer Sparkling Cranberries on a cocktail pick and rest across rim of glass.

Sparkling Cranberries

1 cup light corn syrup

2 cups fresh cranberries

1 cup sparkling sugar or granulated sugar

1. Heat corn syrup in a saucepan over medium-low 1 to 2 minutes. (Caution: If syrup gets too hot cranberries will pop.) Remove from heat; stir in cranberries. Cover and chill 8 to 12 hours.

2. Place sugar in a shallow dish. Drain cranberries in a colander, about 15 minutes. Add 4 to 5 cranberries at a time to sugar; gently toss to coat. Repeat with remaining cranberries. Place cranberries in a single layer on a parchment paper-lined baking sheet; let stand until completely dry. Use immediately or store in an airtight container at room temperature and use within 48 hours. Makes 2 cups.

Pig Pinwheels

MAKES **2 DOZEN**   ACTIVE **35 MIN.**   TOTAL **1 HOUR**

A puff pastry cradle takes pigs-in-a-blanket from ho-humble to holiday heights. Instead of hot dogs or little smokies, we use Conecuh county sausage. Its hickory-smoked flavor makes it a welcome addition to soups and stews, while its narrow size makes slices easier to eat. Conecuh is made in Alabama and sold in grocery stores throughout the South. If you can't find it, substitute your favorite smoked sausage.

1 large egg yolk

½ (17.3-oz) pkg. frozen puff pastry sheets (1 sheet), thawed and cut into 4 rectangles

12 oz. smoked sausage, sliced into ½-inch rounds

Butter

Tomato chutney or pepper jelly

Sliced jalapeños, for garnish (optional)

1. Preheat oven to 375°F. Whisk together egg yolk and 1 tablespoon water in a small bowl. Brush 1 long side of each pastry rectangle with egg mixture. Place 1 sausage along opposite side of each rectangle; roll up, pressing edges to seal. Place in freezer for 15 minutes or until dough is slightly firm.

2. Cut each log crosswise into 6 equal slices. Place 1 slice, cut side down, in each of 24 buttered muffin cups. Bake in preheated oven until pastry is golden and sausage sizzles, about 25 minutes.

3. Drain on paper towels. Serve with tomato chutney or pepper jelly. Garnish with jalapeño slices, if desired.

APRICOT-GORGONZOLA BITES, PAGE 101

PROSCIUTTO-ASPARAGUS WRAPS, PAGE 101

FETA FONDUE,
PAGE 100

SHRIMP COCKTAIL
WITH FIVE-INGREDIENT
COCKTAIL SAUCE,
PAGE 100

RELISH TRAY
SKEWERS,
PAGE 100

Shrimp Cocktail with Five-Ingredient Cocktail Sauce

SERVES **12**   ACTIVE **10 MIN.**   TOTAL **10 MIN.**

Use your favorite Bloody Mary mix to zest up the sauce.

2 ½ lb. cooked, peeled large (16-20 count) shrimp, chilled

1 (12-oz.) bottle chili sauce

3 Tbsp. Bloody Mary mix

2 Tbsp. prepared horseradish

½ tsp. Worcestershire sauce

1 Tbsp. fresh lemon juice

1. Arrange shrimp on a chilled platter.

2. Combine chili sauce, Bloody Mary mix, horseradish, Worcestershire sauce, and lemon juice in a bowl. Serve with shrimp.

Feta Fondue

SERVES **12 TO 16**   ACTIVE **15 MIN.**   TOTAL **20 MIN.**

Feta cubes dunked into a warm marinara sauce are an easy crowd-pleaser.

2 lb. feta cheese, drained and cut into ¾-inch cubes

30 small fresh basil leaves

Cocktail skewers

1 (24-oz) jar marinara sauce

1. Top each feta cube with a basil leaf and secure with a cocktail skewer. Arrange skewers on a platter.

2. Bring marinara sauce to a simmer in a medium saucepan over medium-low, stirring occasionally. Transfer sauce to a chafing dish or fondue pot to keep warm.

3. Dip skewers in warm sauce.

Relish Tray Skewers

MAKES **24**   ACTIVE **15 MIN.**   TOTAL **15 MIN.**

Skewered fresh and pickled veggies are a great palate refresher and add color and pizzazz to any finger-food assortment. Use the larger vegetable pieces from a jar of Italian giardiniera, like the cauliflower florets and carrot chunks. Keep things on the skewer bite-size for easy eating. Don't limit yourself to this list of ingredients. Swap in other favorites like cornichon, marinated mushrooms, or pepperoncini peppers.

24 small pickled okra

24 whole sweet peppadew peppers

24 marinated artichoke hearts

24 grape tomatoes

24 jumbo cheese-stuffed olives

24 marinated giardiniera vegetables

24 cocktail onions

24 radishes

24 (12-inch) bamboo skewers

Thread 1 of each ingredient on each of 24 skewers.

Apricot–Gorgonzola Bites

MAKES **24**   ACTIVE **15 MIN.**   TOTAL **15 MIN.**

This creative combo of sweet-tart dried fruit, blue cheese, pecans, and herbs drizzled with honey is a surprise hit.

2 oz. Gorgonzola cheese, crumbled (about 1/2 cup)

24 dried apricot halves

1/4 cup coarsely chopped toasted pecans

2 Tbsp. honey

1 tsp. chopped fresh thyme

Place 1 teaspoon crumbled cheese on each apricot; top each with 1/2 teaspoon chopped pecans. Drizzle evenly with honey. Sprinkle with thyme.

Prosciutto–Asparagus Wraps

MAKES **36**   ACTIVE **30 MIN.**   TOTAL **30 MIN.**

Sweet, syrupy balsamic glaze is a mouthwatering counterpoint to the salty prosciutto and creamy goat cheese in this two-bite appetizer.

36 asparagus spears

18 slices (about 3/4 lb.) prosciutto

1 (5-oz.) log goat cheese

1 tsp. kosher salt

1 tsp. black pepper

Bottled balsamic glaze

1. Snap off and discard tough ends of asparagus. Cut asparagus tips into 3 1/2-inch spears, reserving tender end portions for another use.

2. Cook asparagus in boiling water to cover until crisp-tender, 1 to 2 minutes; drain. Plunge into ice water to stop the cooking process; drain and pat dry with paper towels.

3. Slice prosciutto in half lengthwise; spread each slice with some goat cheese, sprinkle with a pinch each of salt and pepper, and roll around asparagus spear. Drizzle with balsamic glaze.

Southern-Style Affogato

MAKES **12**   ACTIVE **10 MIN.**   TOTAL **10 MIN.**

Instead of the licorice-flavor sambuca traditionally drizzled over ice cream for affogato, offer a few Southern liqueurs for your guests to choose from to tailor to tastes. Serve with store-bought pirouette cookies.

3 cups coffee ice cream

3 cups brewed strong coffee

12 tablespoons (3/4 cup) coarsely ground espresso beans

3/4 cup liqueur of choice (optional)

Pirouette cookies

Using a small ice cream scoop, portion ice cream into each of 12 heatproof small mugs; top evenly with coffee, espresso beans, and liqueur of choice, if desired. Serve immediately with pirouette cookies.

Southern Liqueurs

Try these boozy regional flavors to spike an after-dinner coffee or drizzle over ice cream.

Herbsaint

Praline Pecan Liqueur

Southern Comfort

Hoodoo Chicory Liqueur

Ole Smoky Mountain Java

Double Shot Coffee Bourbon Cream Liqueur

Jackson Morgan Southern Cream

Nashville Craft Spiced Honey Liqueur

Savor & Share

HOLIDAY COOKBOOK

ENDIVE
AND CRESS
SALAD WITH
BACON-CIDER
DRESSING,
PAGE 108

SAGE-BROWN
BUTTER ROLLS,
PAGE 109

BEET AND
CARROT SOUP,
PAGE 108

Seasonal Starters

*Enjoy more leisurely meals with family and friends
by serving multiple courses instead of
all the dishes at once. These simple starters
are easy, elegant, and whet the appetite
for the main attractions to come.*

Beet and Carrot Soup

SERVES **8**   ACTIVE **20 MIN.**   TOTAL **1 HOUR, 30 MIN.**

This soup is earthy and just sweet enough. Buy untrimmed celery instead of celery hearts so you have the wonderful, mild leaves to use as a garnish.

2 lb. small red beets, peeled and quartered

1 lb. large carrots, peeled and halved lengthwise

5 tsp. olive oil, divided

1/2 tsp. kosher salt

3 cups diced peeled apple

1 cup chopped yellow onion

1/4 cup chopped celery

1 tsp. pumpkin pie spice

4 cups vegetable broth

4 cups water

3 tsp. fresh lemon juice

1 cup plain Greek yogurt

1 cup chopped walnuts, toasted

2/3 cup coarsely chopped celery leaves

1. Preheat oven to 425°F.

2. Line a rimmed baking sheet with parchment paper. Place beets and carrots in a bowl. Drizzle with 3 teaspoons oil; sprinkle with the salt. Toss. Arrange vegetables on prepared pan. Bake in preheated oven until tender, about 40 minutes, stirring once. Remove from oven; cool slightly. Cut beets and carrots into 1-inch pieces.

3. Heat a Dutch oven over medium and add remaining 2 teaspoons oil; swirl to coat. Add apple, onion, celery, and pumpkin pie spice to pot; cook 1½ minutes. Add beet mixture, broth, and the water; bring to a boil. Reduce heat, and simmer 30 minutes. Remove from heat, and let stand 15 minutes.

4. Place beet mixture in a blender in batches, and blend until smooth. Return soup to pot. Stir in lemon juice. Ladle soup into each of 8 bowls; top each serving with 2 tablespoons yogurt, 2 tablespoons walnuts, and 1 tablespoon celery leaves.

QUICK TIP: *Find cooked, peeled beets in vacuum-packed bags in the produce section of most supermarkets.*

Endive and Cress Salad with Bacon-Cider Dressing

SERVES **6**   ACTIVE **25 MIN.**   TOTAL **25 MIN.**

A rainbow of lettuces lends color, crunch, and contrast. Smoky bacon, tangy Dijon mustard, and maple syrup temper the peppery bite of the bitter greens.

4 center-cut bacon slices

3 Tbsp. extra virgin olive oil

2½ Tbsp. cider vinegar

2 Tbsp. maple syrup

1 tsp. coarse-ground Dijon mustard

1/4 tsp. kosher salt

1/4 tsp. black pepper

1 garlic clove, minced

4 cups (1/2-inch) diagonally cut Belgian endive

3 cups chopped radicchio

1 cup trimmed watercress

2 oz. Gorgonzola cheese, crumbled (about 1/2 cup)

1/2 cup toasted chopped pecans

1. Heat a medium nonstick skillet over medium. Add bacon to pan; cook until crisp, 5 to 7 minutes. Remove bacon from pan, reserving 2 teaspoons drippings; coarsely chop bacon.

2. Combine reserved drippings, oil, vinegar, maple syrup, mustard, salt, pepper, and garlic in a large bowl, stirring with a whisk. Add endive, radicchio, watercress, cheese, and pecans; toss well. Sprinkle with chopped bacon.

Sage-Brown Butter Rolls

SERVES **8**   ACTIVE **10 MIN.**   TOTAL **30 MIN.**

Use store-bought refrigerated bread dough to make pretty knotted rolls that you can gussy up with your favorite toppings.

1 (13.2-oz.) pkg. refrigerated French bread dough

Flour, for dusting

1½ Tbsp. unsalted butter

2 tsp. finely chopped fresh sage

2 garlic cloves, minced

⅛ tsp. kosher salt

1. Preheat oven to 350°F.

2. Place dough on a lightly floured surface; dust dough with flour. Cut dough in half crosswise; cut each half lengthwise into 4 strips to form 8 strips total. Working with 1 strip at a time, stretch strip gently to extend length; tie in a knot, tucking ends under. Arrange knots 3 inches apart on a parchment paper–lined baking sheet.

3. Bake rolls in preheated oven until golden, about 20 minutes.

4. While rolls bake, melt butter in a small skillet. Cook until bubbly and lightly browned, about 2 minutes. Add sage and garlic to pan; cook until fragrant, about 1 minute. Brush butter mixture over hot rolls; sprinkle evenly with salt.

Curried Butternut Soup

SERVES **8**   ACTIVE **25 MIN.**   TOTAL **1 HOUR, 20 MIN.**

The exotic notes of coconut and red curry pair beautifully with earthy butternut squash in this creamy bisque. Top with chopped sweet red bell pepper if you want a pretty pop of color in the garnish minus the heat.

1 (2½-lb.) butternut squash, peeled, seeded, and cut into 2-inch cubes

1 Tbsp. plus 1 tsp. canola oil, divided

¾ tsp. kosher salt, divided

1 cup chopped onion

3 cups no-salt-added chicken stock

4 tsp. red curry paste

1½ Tbsp. fresh lime juice

1 (13.5-oz.) can light coconut milk

¼ cup fresh cilantro leaves

¼ cup flaked unsweetened coconut, toasted

2 small Thai red chiles, thinly sliced

1. Preheat oven to 450°F.

2. Line a rimmed baking sheet with parchment paper. Place squash in a bowl, and drizzle with 1 tablespoon oil. Sprinkle with ¼ teaspoon salt, and toss. Bake in preheated oven until golden and tender, about 35 minutes.

3. Heat remaining 1 teaspoon oil in a large saucepan over medium; swirl to coat. Add onion; cook 5 minutes, stirring occasionally. Add squash mixture, stock, and curry paste. Sprinkle with remaining ½ teaspoon salt, and bring to a boil. Reduce heat, and simmer 15 minutes, stirring occasionally. Remove from heat; stir in lime juice and coconut milk. Let stand 15 minutes.

4. Place half of squash mixture in a blender, and blend until smooth. Pour soup into a bowl. Repeat. Divide soup evenly among 8 bowls, and top evenly with cilantro, coconut, and chile slices.

QUICK TIP: *Look for peeled and cubed butternut squash in the freezer section to save time on prep.*

Celery and Herb Salad with Pomegranate Seeds

SERVES **12**   ACTIVE **10 MIN.**   TOTAL **2 HOURS, 10 MIN.**

Buy bunches of celery with the leaves intact. Use the yellow-green leaves to add contrasting color and a subtle celery flavor to salads.

⅔ cup pomegranate arils

7 cups thinly diagonally sliced celery (including leaves)

3 cups loosely packed fresh flat-leaf parsley leaves

1 cup loosely packed fresh mint leaves, torn

¼ tsp. kosher salt

½ tsp. black pepper

3 Tbsp. white balsamic vinegar

¼ cup extra virgin olive oil

1. Combine pomegranate arils, celery, parsley, and mint in a large bowl.

2. In small jar with a lid, combine salt, pepper, vinegar, and olive oil. Cover and shake vigorously until emulsified. Drizzle dressing over salad; toss gently to coat. Cover; refrigerate at least 2 hours.

Soup Toppers

Try these fun garnishes to add flavorful wow factor to any soup:

Toasted seeds and nuts
Pomegranate arils
Fresh herb leaves or microgreens
Croutons
Tortilla strips
Crumbled or shaved cheese
Diced or sliced avocado
Sour cream or plain Greek yogurt
Minced or sliced jalapeño
Crumbled bacon
Chopped scallions
Pesto
Pico de gallo
Crackers and crumbs
Crumbled cheese crisps

OYSTERS
TWO WAYS:
BROILED WITH
GARLIC-BUTTER
BREADCRUMBS,
PAGE 115

SHRIMP CAKES WITH
ROASTED GARLIC SAUCE,
PAGE 114

AVOCADOS
STUFFED
WITH CRAB,
PAGE 114

OYSTERS TWO WAYS:
RAW WITH PINK
PEPPERCORN
MIGNONETTE,
PAGE 115

Shrimp Cakes with Roasted Garlic Sauce

SERVES **8**   ACTIVE **35 MIN.**   TOTAL **1 HOUR, 25 MIN.**

Substitute Great Northern or navy beans if you can't find cannellini beans.

1 whole garlic head

2 Tbsp. plus 1 tsp. olive oil, divided

1/2 cup plain Greek yogurt

1 tsp. fresh lime juice

1/2 tsp. black pepper, divided

1/4 tsp. kosher salt, divided

1/2 lb. peeled and deveined medium shrimp

1 (15-oz.) can cannellini beans, rinsed and drained, divided

1/2 cup cooked bulgur

1/4 cup coarsely chopped fresh parsley leaves

4 cups arugula leaves

1. Preheat oven to 375°F.

2. Remove white papery skin from garlic head (do not peel or separate cloves). Drizzle 1 teaspoon oil over garlic; wrap in foil. Bake in preheated oven 1 hour; cool 10 minutes. Separate cloves; squeeze into a small bowl to extract pulp. Discard skins. Mash garlic using back of a spoon. Stir in yogurt, juice, 1/4 teaspoon pepper, and 1/8 teaspoon salt.

3. Place 3 shrimp and 2/3 cup beans in a food processor; pulse until blended but not quite pureed. Add remaining shrimp and beans, the bulgur, parsley, and remaining 1/4 teaspoon pepper and 1/8 teaspoon salt to food processor; pulse until coarsely chopped. Drop 2 tablespoons mixture onto a platter lined with parchment paper; gently pat into a 1-inch-wide patty. Repeat procedure with remaining shrimp mixture, forming 8 cakes. Refrigerate 20 minutes.

4. Preheat broiler to high and brush a jelly-roll pan with 1 tablespoon oil. Arrange chilled cakes on pan; brush tops of cakes with remaining 1 tablespoon oil. Broil 5 minutes or until browned. Carefully turn cakes over. Brush tops of cakes with oil from pan. Broil an additional 5 minutes or until browned.

5. Divide arugula leaves among 8 salad plates. Top with cakes and serve with sauce.

Avocados Stuffed with Crab

SERVES **8**   ACTIVE **10 MIN.**   TOTAL **10 MIN.**

Sweet crabmeat dressed with zingy lemon and tarragon is a nice complement to buttery avocado. Chopped cooked shrimp or shredded chicken breast would also work here.

1 cup mayonnaise

1 tsp. lemon zest

1/2 cup fresh lemon juice

6 Tbsp. chopped fresh cilantro

1 tsp. black pepper

24 oz. lump crabmeat, shell pieces removed

Cooking spray

4 ripe avocados, halved and pitted

1/2 cup microgreens

1. Combine mayonnaise, lemon zest and juice, cilantro, and pepper in a bowl; gently fold in crab.

2. Heat a large cast-iron skillet over medium-high. Coat pan with cooking spray. Place avocado halves, cut sides down, in pan; cook until lightly browned, about 2 minutes.

3. Place avocado halves, cut sides down, on a cutting board; cut a very small slice from bottom of each half so that it stands flat. Turn over; spoon about 1/2 cup crab mixture into each avocado half and top with microgreens.

Oysters Two Ways

MAKES **3 DOZEN** ACTIVE **20 MIN.** TOTAL **25 MIN.**

Oysters are at their delicious best in winter; they spawn in the summer and by winter are fat and sweet. This raw and broiled oyster pairing is an elegant start to any meal. Spread a layer of rock salt on each serving plate as a nod to the ocean that also stabilizes the shells.

3 dozen shucked raw oysters on half shells

Pink Peppercorn Mignonette (recipe follows)

Garlic-Butter Breadcrumbs (recipe follows)

Cooking spray

Rock salt

1. Preheat broiler to high. Set aside 18 raw oysters on half shells and keep chilled.

2. Prepare Pink Peppercorn Mignonette and set aside.

3. Prepare Garlic Butter Breadcrumbs.

4. Arrange remaining oysters on a broiler pan coated with cooking spray; top with breadcrumb mixture. Broil 5 inches from heat until breadcrumbs are golden, about 3 minutes. Sprinkle with parsley.

5. Arrange broiled and raw oysters on platters or individual plates covered with a layer of rock salt. Spoon Pink Peppercorn Mignonette over raw oysters. Serve immediately.

Pink Peppercorn Mignonette

1/2 cup champagne vinegar or white wine vinegar

2 Tbsp. finely chopped shallots

2 tsp. pink peppercorns, coarsely crushed

1 1/2 tsp. finely chopped fresh tarragon

1. Combine vinegar, shallots, peppercorns, and tarragon in a bowl; chill until ready to serve.

Garlic-Butter Breadcrumbs

1 Tbsp. butter

2 tsp. extra virgin olive oil

2 garlic cloves, minced

1 tsp. fresh lemon juice

1 (2-oz.) slice French bread baguette

1/8 tsp. salt

1/8 tsp. black pepper

1 Tbsp. chopped fresh parsley

1. Melt butter in a skillet over medium. Add oil and garlic; cook 1 minute, stirring occasionally. Remove from heat, and stir in lemon juice.

2. Place bread in a food processor; pulse 10 times or until coarse crumbs measure 1 cup. Combine breadcrumbs, butter mixture, salt, pepper, and parsley; mix well.

Southern Oysters

The Southeastern United States is becoming a Napa Valley of oysters thanks to cutting-edge aquaculture techniques that cultivate oysters in cages—some that float just above the ocean floor. Like terroir for fine wine, oysters develop a unique flavor profile from the sea water in which they are grown. Some Southern oysters include: Murder Point (Alabama), Salty Birds (Florida), McIntosh (Georgia), Bright Side (Louisiana), Snow Hill (Maryland), French Hermit (Mississippi), Sea Level Salts (North Carolina), Single Lady (South Carolina), Elm Grove (Texas), and Chunus (Virginia).

ROASTED ROMANESCO
AND CAULIFLOWER WITH
GARLIC-ANCHOVY SAUCE,
PAGE 118

Winter Vegetables

Cool-season vegetables are the stars of every side-dish lineup this time of year. These jewels of the plate are tasty, colorful ways to round out any holiday menu.

Roasted Romanesco and Cauliflower with Garlic-Anchovy Sauce

SERVES **6**   ACTIVE **10 MIN.**   TOTAL **45 MIN.**

The sauce nestles into the cracks and crevices of this vegetable duo, infusing this beautiful side dish with zesty, complex flavor. Don't skip the anchovy. Like Worcestershire or soy sauce in other dishes, it lends a meaty, umami note without any fishiness.

1/4 cup extra virgin olive oil

4 oil-packed anchovy fillets, drained

2 garlic cloves, minced

1/4 tsp. crushed red pepper

4 cups Romanesco florets (about 1/2 large head)

4 cups cauliflower florets (about 1/2 large head)

Cooking spray

2 Tbsp. minced fresh flat-leaf parsley

2 tsp. fresh lemon juice

1/4 tsp. kosher salt

Shaved Parmigiano-Reggiano cheese, for garnish (optional)

1. Preheat oven to 450°F.

2. Combine olive oil, anchovies, garlic, and crushed red pepper in a small skillet over medium. Cook until anchovies have broken down, about 5 minutes. Remove pan from heat.

3. Spread Romanesco cauliflower in a single layer on a baking sheet coated with cooking spray. Coat vegetables with cooking spray. Bake in preheated oven 10 minutes. Drizzle oil mixture over vegetables; toss to coat. Bake until edges are browned, about 25 minutes, stirring once after 15 minutes. Sprinkle with parsley, lemon juice, and salt. Garnish with cheese, if desired.

Mashed Potatoes and Parsnips

SERVES **12**   ACTIVE **30 MIN.**   TOTAL **55 MIN.**

Adding another vegetable to mashed potatoes is a nice change of pace. Sweet, earthy parsnips add distinctive flavor here.

3/4 cup butter

3 lb. Yukon gold potatoes, peeled and cut into large chunks

2 lb. parsnips, peeled and cut into large chunks

1/4 medium-size onion

6 garlic cloves, peeled

2 fresh rosemary sprigs

2 bay leaves

3 Tbsp. kosher salt

1/2 cup chicken broth

1/2 cup buttermilk

Chopped fresh chives, for garnish

1. Cook butter in a 2-quart heavy saucepan over medium, stirring constantly, just until butter begins to turn golden brown, 6 to 8 minutes. Immediately remove pan from heat, and pour butter into a small bowl. (Butter will continue to darken if left in saucepan.)

2. Bring potatoes, parsnips, onion, garlic, rosemary, bay leaves, salt, and enough water to cover to a boil in a stockpot over medium-high. Cook until tender, 25 to 30 minutes. Drain. Remove and discard herb stems and bay leaves. Return potato mixture to pot. Mash with a potato masher to desired consistency.

3. Stir in broth, buttermilk, and all but 2 tablespoons of the browned butter until just blended. Serve topped with remaining browned butter and chives.

ROASTED RADICCHIO
WITH PANCETTA
AND PINE NUTS,
PAGE 122

MUSHROOM
CARPACCIO WITH
GREMOLATA
AND SHAVED
PARMIGIANO,
PAGE 122

ROASTED RAINBOW
CARROTS WITH
CARROT TOP-HERB
GREMOLATA,
PAGE 123

HONEY-ROASTED
BRUSSELS SPROUTS
PAGE 123

Roasted Radicchio with Pancetta and Pine Nuts

SERVES **8**   ACTIVE **20 MIN.**   TOTAL **35 MIN.**

Radicchio—that bitter, crunchy, ruby-and-white vegetable Italians adore—becomes entirely different when roasted. Its color deepens and the flavor turns mellow and nutty, with just a hint of bitterness remaining. Serve it alongside roast pork, chicken, or beef. Or, to turn it into a main course, chop and toss with hot cooked pasta.

2 Tbsp. extra virgin olive oil

1 Tbsp. chopped fresh thyme

1/2 tsp. kosher salt

1/2 tsp. black pepper

3 medium heads radicchio, quartered

2 oz. thinly sliced pancetta

1 large shallot, thinly sliced

1/4 cup pine nuts, toasted

1 Tbsp. red wine vinegar

2 tsp. pure maple syrup

Fresh thyme sprigs, for garnish (optional)

1. Preheat oven to 400°F.

2. Combine oil, chopped thyme, salt, pepper, and radicchio on a rimmed baking sheet; toss to coat. Bake in preheated oven until wilted and slightly charred, about 20 minutes.

3. Meanwhile, cook pancetta in a large skillet over medium until browned and crisp, about 10 minutes, stirring occasionally. Remove pancetta from pan; coarsely crumble. Add shallot to pan; cook until lightly browned, about 3 minutes. Arrange radicchio on a platter. Sprinkle pancetta, shallot, and pine nuts over radicchio. Drizzle with vinegar and maple syrup. Garnish with thyme sprigs, if desired.

Mushroom Carpaccio with Gremolata and Shaved Parmigiano

SERVES **6**   ACTIVE **20 MIN.**   TOTAL **35 MIN.**

This salad is the perfect antidote to the winter blues, and it pairs beautifully with foods of the season—roasts, stews, and braises. You could use a mandoline to slice the mushrooms, but a sharp knife will do.

3 large button mushrooms (about 2 1/2 to 3 inches in diameter)

3 large cremini mushrooms (about 2 1/2 to 3 inches in diameter)

1 cup fresh flat-leaf parsley leaves, finely chopped

1 Tbsp. lemon zest

2 garlic cloves, minced

3 Tbsp. fresh lemon juice

1/4 tsp. kosher salt

1/4 tsp. coarsely ground white pepper, plus more for garnish

3 Tbsp. extra virgin olive oil

1 oz. Parmigiano-Reggiano cheese, shaved (about 2 Tbsp.)

1. Gently wash and dry mushrooms. Trim very bottom ends of mushrooms, leaving stems intact. Cut mushrooms vertically into very thin slices; arrange on a platter so they overlap slightly.

2. Combine parsley, lemon zest, and garlic in a bowl. In a small jar with a lid, combine lemon juice, salt, pepper, and oil. Cover and shake vigorously until emulsified. Drizzle dressing evenly over mushrooms; sprinkle with parsley mixture and cheese. Let stand at room temperature at least 15 minutes before serving.

Roasted Rainbow Carrots with Carrot Top-Herb Gremolata

SERVES **6 TO 8**   ACTIVE **10 MIN.**   TOTAL **45 MIN.**

Carrots become sweetly caramelized and candylike in the heat of a blasting-hot oven.

3 lb. small rainbow carrots with tops, scrubbed

1 Tbsp. olive oil

³/₄ tsp. kosher salt

¹/₄ tsp. black pepper

2 Tbsp. chopped fresh carrot tops

2 Tbsp. finely chopped fresh flat-leaf parsley

2 Tbsp. finely chopped fresh mint

1 Tbsp. lemon zest

3 garlic cloves, minced

1. Preheat oven to 450°F. Peel carrots, if desired. Trim tops to 1 inch, reserving tops.

2. Toss carrots with oil, salt, and pepper, and place on a 17- x 12-inch jelly-roll pan. Roast in preheated oven 20 minutes, stirring once. Reduce heat to 325°F, and roast, stirring occasionally, until carrots are browned and tender, about 15 minutes.

3. For the gremolata, combine carrot tops, parsley, mint, lemon zest, and garlic in a small bowl. Spoon gremolata over roasted carrots and serve warm.

Honey-Roasted Brussels Sprouts

SERVES **8**   ACTIVE **10 MIN.**   TOTAL **50 MIN.**

Honey tempers the bitterness of the Brussels sprouts.

2 lb. Brussels sprouts, trimmed, cut in half

¹/₄ cup olive oil

Kosher salt and black pepper

¹/₄ cup honey

1 cup dried cherries

¹/₂ cup sliced almonds

1. Preheat oven to 350°F. Combine Brussels sprouts and oil in a large bowl. Season with salt and pepper to taste; toss to coat.

2. Spread on a rimmed baking sheet in a single layer, cut side down, and roast until tender and edges are starting to brown, about 35 minutes.

3. Drizzle Brussels sprouts with honey and sprinkle evenly with dried cherries and almonds. Bake until warmed through, about 5 minutes.

Winter Wonders

A world of hearty, cool-season greens abound this time of year. Add some to your cooking all season long.

Arugula, bok choy, broccoli raab, cabbage, collards, kale, mustard greens, tatsoi, and turnip greens are distinctively flavored cruciferous varieties packed with nutrients.

Beet greens, spinach, and Swiss chard are members of the amaranth family with a tender texture and milder flavor.

Endive, escarole, frisée, and radicchio are members of the chicory family that are sturdy-leaved with a pleasing bitterness.

Green Beans with Bacon and Breadcrumbs

SERVES 6   ACTIVE **55 MIN.**   TOTAL **55 MIN.**

Go beyond the can-of-this and can-of-that creamy casserole iteration and serve up this fresh take on a holiday classic.

1 lb. haricots verts (French green beans), trimmed

6 thick-cut bacon slices

1½ cups torn sourdough bread (from 1 [1-lb.] loaf)

1 medium-size yellow onion, thinly sliced (about 2 cups)

1 Tbsp. canola oil

1 cup heavy cream

1 tsp. kosher salt

⅛ tsp. black pepper

1. Bring a large pot of salted water to a boil over high. Add green beans; cook until tender-crisp, 3 to 5 minutes. Drain; rinse with cold water. Drain; set aside.

2. Cook bacon in a 10-inch skillet over medium-high, stirring occasionally, until crisp, about 10 minutes. Remove from heat. Transfer bacon to a plate lined with paper towels, reserving drippings in skillet. Pulse bread pieces in a food processor until breadcrumbs form, about 20 pulses. (You'll have about 1 cup.) Add breadcrumbs to drippings in skillet. Cook over medium, stirring often, until golden brown and dry to touch, about 8 minutes. Remove from skillet; set aside.

3. Add onion and oil to skillet over medium-high. Cook, stirring often, until browned, about 15 minutes. Add cream, salt, and pepper, stirring up browned bits on bottom of skillet. Bring to a boil over medium-high. Reduce heat to medium. Cook, stirring often, until liquid thickens, about 5 minutes. Stir in green beans. Crumble bacon over mixture, and stir to combine. Transfer mixture to a shallow dish or platter. Sprinkle with breadcrumbs.

ANDOUILLE
MAC-N-CHEESE,
PAGE 128

Starches & Grains

*Find comfort digging into a bowl of warm,
gooey mac-n-cheese or a toothsome,
nutty accompaniment of wild rice or quinoa.
Pairing these sides with protein or
vegetables delivers hearty, satisfying meals.*

Andouille Mac-n-Cheese

SERVES **12** ACTIVE **35 MIN.** TOTAL **1 HOUR**

Potato chips are the secret to the crispy crust.

1 (16-oz.) pkg. uncooked cavatappi pasta

1 Tbsp. kosher salt

1/2 lb. andouille sausage, casings removed

4 cups heavy cream

1 (16-oz.) pkg. processed cheese, cut into 1-inch cubes

8 oz. smoked cheddar cheese, shredded (about 2 cups)

2 oz. aged Gouda cheese, grated (about 1/2 cup)

2 oz. Parmigiano-Reggiano cheese, grated (about 1/2 cup)

1 (5-oz.) pkg. unsalted kettle-cooked potato chips, crumbled

1. Preheat oven to 375˚F. Prepare pasta according package directions for al dente, adding salt to water.

2. Cut sausage lengthwise into quarters. Cut each quarter into ¼-inch-thick pieces. Sauté in a Dutch oven over medium until browned at edges, about 3 minutes; drain on paper towels.

3. Simmer cream in Dutch oven over medium–high; reduce heat to low. Stir in processed cheese, stirring constantly, until melted. Add sausage and remaining cheeses. Cook, stirring constantly, until melted. Stir in hot cooked pasta.

4. Pour into 12 (8-oz.) buttered ramekins; top with potato chips. Bake in preheated oven until browned, about 20 minutes.

More than Macaroni

Swap in one of these pasta shapes for the usual macaroni in your favorite recipe.

Campanelle	Penne
Cavatappi	Fusilli
Conchiglie or shell pasta	Radiatori
	Rotini
Farfalle or bowties	Rotelle or
Orecchiette	wagon wheels

Sweet Potato Stacks

SERVES **12** ACTIVE **25 MIN.** TOTAL **1 HOUR, 5 MIN.**

Like side-dish Napoleons, these savory stacks are creamy, rich, and oh-so-elegant paired with roasted meats or fish.

1½ lb. small sweet potatoes, peeled and thinly sliced

2 tsp. chopped fresh thyme, divided

2 oz. Gruyère cheese, shredded, divided (about 1/2 cup)

2 oz. Parmesan cheese, grated (about 1/2 cup)

2/3 cup heavy cream

1 garlic clove, minced

1/2 to 3/4 tsp. kosher salt

1/4 tsp. black pepper

Fresh thyme leaves, for garnish (optional)

1. Preheat oven to 375˚F. Layer half of the sweet potatoes in a lightly greased 12-cup muffin pan. Sprinkle with 1½ teaspoons chopped thyme, ¼ cup Gruyère, and ¼ cup Parmesan. Top with remaining sweet potatoes. (Potatoes will come slightly above rim of each cup.)

2. Microwave cream, garlic, salt, pepper, and remaining ½ teaspoon chopped thyme at HIGH 1 minute. Pour cream mixture into muffin cups (about 1 tablespoon per cup).

3. Cover with aluminum foil, and bake in preheated oven 30 minutes. Uncover and sprinkle with remaining ¼ cup Gruyère and ¼ cup Parmesan. Bake until cheese is melted and slightly golden, 5 to 7 minutes

4. Let stand 5 minutes. Run a sharp knife around rim of each cup, and lift potato stacks from cups using a spoon or thin spatula. Transfer to a serving platter and garnish with thyme leaves, if desired.

CARROT ORZO,
PAGE 133

QUINOA WITH
TOASTED PECANS,
PAGE 132

WILD RICE
WITH APPLES,
PAGE 132

PISTACHIO-
POMEGRANATE RICE,
PAGE 133

Quinoa with Toasted Pecans

SERVES **6**   ACTIVE **15 MIN.**   TOTAL **25 MIN.**

Quinoa is all the rage these days, and toasted pecans and herbs make this hearty whole grain extra delicious.

1 cup uncooked red and white quinoa blend

1 Tbsp. plus 2 tsp. extra virgin olive oil, divided

2 Tbsp. finely chopped shallots

3 garlic cloves, minced

1¼ cups unsalted chicken stock

¼ tsp. kosher salt

¼ cup coarsely chopped toasted pecans

¼ cup chopped fresh parsley

2 Tbsp. chopped fresh chives

¼ tsp. black pepper

1. Rinse and drain quinoa. Heat a large saucepan over medium–high. Add 2 teaspoons olive oil to pan; swirl to coat. Add shallots; sauté 1 minute or until tender. Add garlic; cook 1 minute, stirring constantly. Add quinoa; cook 2 minutes, stirring frequently. Add chicken stock and salt; bring to a boil. Cover, reduce heat, and simmer until liquid is absorbed and quinoa is tender, about 13 minutes.

2. While quinoa cooks, heat a large nonstick skillet over medium. Add pecans to pan; cook until browned, about 3 minutes, stirring frequently. Combine quinoa mixture, pecans, remaining 1 tablespoon olive oil, the parsley, chives, and pepper; toss.

Wild Rice with Apples

SERVES **8**   ACTIVE **20 MIN.**   TOTAL **1 HOUR, 20 MIN.**

If Pink Lady apples aren't available, use any crisp, sweet apple, such as Honeycrisp or Macoun, or try an heirloom variety.

2 Tbsp. butter, divided

2 cups chopped Pink Lady apples

1 cup chopped leek

2 garlic cloves, minced

3 cups fat-free, less-sodium chicken broth

1 cup apple cider

1 tsp. chopped fresh thyme

2 cups uncooked wild rice

⅓ cup chopped pecans, toasted

¾ tsp. kosher salt

½ tsp. black pepper

1. Melt 1 tablespoon butter in a large saucepan over medium–high. Add apples; sauté until tender and lightly browned, about 7 minutes. Remove from pan.

2. Reduce heat to medium. Melt remaining 1 tablespoon butter in pan. Add leek; cook until tender, about 5 minutes, stirring occasionally. Add garlic; cook 30 seconds, stirring occasionally. Stir in broth, 2 cups water, the cider, and thyme; bring to a boil. Stir in rice; reduce heat, and simmer 55 minutes or until liquid is absorbed. Drain and discard excess liquid. Return rice mixture to pan over medium. Stir in apples, pecans, salt, and pepper; cook until heated through, about 2 minutes.

Pistachio–Pomegranate Rice

SERVES **6**   ACTIVE **5 MIN.**   TOTAL **25 MIN.**

Green pistachios and ruby pomegranate arils add a colorful holiday accent to this simple side dish.

2 cups water

1 cup uncooked basmati rice

3/4 tsp. kosher salt, divided

2 Tbsp. pomegranate arils

1 1/2 Tbsp. chopped pistachios

1 Tbsp. chopped fresh flat-leaf parsley

2 Tbsp. pistachio oil

1/4 tsp. black pepper

Fresh parsley sprigs, for garnish (optional)

Bring the water to a boil in a medium saucepan; add rice and 1/4 teaspoon salt. Cover, reduce heat, and simmer 18 minutes, or until liquid is absorbed and rice is done. Remove from heat; fluff with a fork. Add remaining 1/2 teaspoon salt, the pomegranate arils, pistachios, parsley, pistachio oil, and pepper. Cover; let stand 5 minutes. Garnish with parsley sprigs, if desired.

Carrot Orzo

SERVES **6 TO 8**   ACTIVE **40 MIN.**   TOTAL **40 MIN.**

8 oz. carrots, cut into 1-inch pieces (about 2 cups)

2 1/2 cups chicken broth

3 Tbsp. butter

1 medium-size onion, chopped

2 cups uncooked orzo pasta

2 garlic cloves, minced

1 tsp. kosher salt

1/2 tsp. black pepper

4 oz. Parmesan cheese, grated (about 1 cup)

3 Tbsp. chopped fresh chives

1 tsp. chopped fresh thyme

Carrot curls, for garnish (optional)

1. Process carrots in a food processor until finely chopped, about 15 seconds.

2. Combine 2 1/2 cups water and the broth in a microwave-safe measuring cup. Microwave at HIGH 5 minutes or until very hot.

3. Meanwhile, melt butter in a large saucepan over medium. Add chopped carrots and onion, and cook until tender, about 5 minutes, stirring occasionally. Add orzo and garlic, and cook about 1 minute.

4. Slowly stir hot broth mixture, salt, and pepper into orzo mixture. Cook, stirring often, until liquid is absorbed, 15 to 18 minutes.

5. Stir in cheese, chives, and thyme until blended. Garnish with carrot curls, if desired.

CAJUN ÉTOUFFÉE,
PAGE 136

Main Attractions

*Draw them in with these showstopping
Southern recipes that are sophisticated enough
for the holidays and company-worthy
the rest of the year.*

Cajun Étouffée

SERVES **12**   ACTIVE **45 MIN.**   TOTAL **50 MIN.**

This classic crawfish dish starts with a simply seasoned roux. Enriched with crawfish fat, the recipe closely resembles the original 1920s dish created by Mrs. Charles Hebert at the eponymous Breaux Bridge Hebert Hotel. Adding tomatoes to the mix would make this Creole Étouffée. This is a great option for an easy but elegant Christmas Eve dinner.

4 (1-lb.) pkg. peeled crawfish tails with fat

1 Tbsp. hot sauce

1 tsp. cayenne pepper

1/2 cup vegetable oil

1/2 cup all-purpose flour

4 celery ribs, chopped

2 large onions, chopped

3 large green bell peppers, chopped

1 bunch scallions with tops, chopped

1 tsp. kosher salt

1/2 tsp. black pepper

1/2 cup chopped fresh flat-leaf parsley

1/4 cup heavy cream

Hot cooked rice

1. Sprinkle crawfish with hot sauce and ¼ to ½ teaspoon cayenne pepper.

2. Stir together oil and flour in a 4-quart Dutch oven. Cook over medium, stirring constantly, until roux is golden brown, 10 to 15 minutes.

3. Stir in celery, onions, green peppers, and scallions; cook, stirring often, until vegetables are tender, about 8 minutes. Add crawfish and ½ cup water; cook over low, stirring occasionally, 15 minutes.

4. Stir in salt, black pepper, and remaining ½ teaspoon cayenne pepper; simmer 5 minutes. Stir in parsley and cream. Serve over rice.

Cornish Game Hens

SERVES **6**   ACTIVE **30 MIN.**   TOTAL **1 HOUR, 30 MIN.**

Serve this dish family style on a large platter, or plate hens individually. Either way, be sure to warm your serving dishes in advance.

6 (1- to 1½-lb.) Cornish game hens, rinsed and patted dry

4½ tsp. kosher salt, divided

2 tsp. black pepper, divided

2 clementines, unpeeled and quartered, plus more for garnish

6 fresh sage leave, plus more for garnish

3 Tbsp. butter, softened

Kumquats, halved, for garnish

1. Preheat oven to 450°F. Season each hen cavity with ½ teaspoon salt and ¼ teaspoon pepper, and insert 1 clementine quarter into each.

2. Pull back breast skin of each hen gently, and insert 1 sage leaf. Replace skin, and use a presoaked wooden pick to secure skin to meat. Tuck wing tips under each hen, and tie legs together using butcher's twine.

3. Arrange hens, tail to tail in 2 rows, on a rimmed baking sheet, making sure wing tips stay tucked. Rub hens with butter, and season with remaining 1½ teaspoons salt and ½ teaspoon. pepper.

4. Roast hens on middle rack in preheated oven until hens are golden brown and reach an internal temperature of 160°F, 45 to 50 minutes. Transfer hens to a rack set over a platter, and cover loosely with heavy-duty aluminum foil. Allow hens to rest 5 minutes before serving. Garnish with additional clementine quarters, kumquats, and sage.

To Truss or Not to Truss

While it's not a must, trussing a bird helps it cook evenly and hold its shape for serving. If you choose not to truss, hot air in the oven more easily enters the cavity, drying out the breast meat from inside and out. For a moist, succulent bird that tastes as good as it looks, opting to truss is always a plus!

Grillades and Grits

SERVES **8**   ACTIVE **1 HOUR, 25 MIN.**
TOTAL **2 HOURS, 30 MIN., INCLUDING GRITS**

2 lb. (¼-inch-thick) pork loin cutlets

1 tsp. kosher salt

½ tsp. black pepper

2 Tbsp. olive oil

¼ cup finely chopped shallots or onion

3 to 4 tsp. chopped fresh thyme

½ cup dry white wine

⅓ cup tomato chutney

2 medium tomatoes, diced

Fresh thyme leaves and sliced scallions, for garnish (optional)

Ham Hock Grits (recipe follows)

1. Preheat oven to 200°F. Season pork with salt and pepper. Cook, in batches, in hot oil in a large skillet over medium–high 3 minutes on each side or until done. Transfer pork to a wire rack in a jelly-roll pan, and keep warm in oven.

2. Add shallots and thyme to skillet; sauté 1 minute or until tender. Stir in wine and tomato chutney until smooth. Stir in tomatoes, and cook 2 to 3 minutes. Add additional salt and pepper to taste. Pour sauce over pork, and garnish with thyme and scallions, if desired. Serve with grits.

Ham Hock Grits

1 Tbsp. olive oil

1½ cups chopped sweet onion

2 garlic cloves, minced

1 ham hock

2 cups uncooked stone-ground grits

1. Heat oil in a large saucepan over medium–high. Cook onion and garlic in hot oil until onion is tender, about 5 minutes. Add ham hock and 8½ cups water to saucepan, and bring to a boil over medium–high. Reduce heat to low and simmer 15 minutes.

2. Stir uncooked grits into simmering water in saucepan; return to a boil, stirring occasionally. Cover, reduce heat to low, and cook, stirring occasionally, until tender, 30 to 35 minutes. Remove ham hock.

BEEF TENDERLOIN
WITH ONION CONFIT,
PAGE 142

Beef Tenderloin with Onion Confit

SERVES **8** ACTIVE **45 MIN.**

TOTAL **1 HOUR, 25 MIN., INCLUDING SAUCE**

This is tenderloin perfection. Caramelized in cognac and pan drippings, the onion confit makes it all the more sublime.

1 (3½-lb.) beef tenderloin, trimmed	2 bunches scallions, chopped
1½ tsp. kosher salt	2 cups chopped shallots
1 tsp. black pepper	5 garlic cloves, minced
2 Tbsp. canola oil	½ cup cognac
3 Tbsp. butter	½ cup beef broth
2 yellow onions, sliced	Horseradish Sauce (recipe follows)
2 large red onions, sliced	

1. Preheat oven to 400°F. Sprinkle beef with ½ teaspoon salt and ½ teaspoon pepper. Tie with kitchen string at 1-inch intervals. Brown on all sides in hot oil in a roasting pan or Dutch oven. Remove beef, reserving drippings in pan.

2. Add butter to hot drippings; cook over medium–high until melted. Add yellow and red onions and remaining salt and pepper; cook 5 minutes. Add scallions, shallots, and garlic; cook 10 minutes. Remove from heat. Add cognac and broth, and return to heat. Cook, stirring constantly, until liquid evaporates, about 5 minutes. Place beef on top of onion mixture.

3. Bake, covered, in preheated oven until a meat thermometer registers 135°F (medium-rare), about 35 minutes. Remove beef from pan; reserve onion mixture. Cover beef loosely and let stand for 10 minutes.

4. Meanwhile, cook onion mixture over medium, stirring constantly, until liquid evaporates, 3 to 5 minutes. Add salt and pepper to taste. Slice beef, and serve with onion mixture.

Horseradish Sauce

Fold together 1⅓ cups sour cream, ½ cup whipping cream (whipped to soft peaks), 6 Tbsp. prepared horseradish, 1½ tsp. Dijon mustard, 3 tsp. fresh lemon juice, and ½ tsp. sugar. Season with kosher salt and black pepper to taste. Makes 2 cups.

Italian Pot Roast

SERVES **6** ACTIVE **20 MIN.** TOTAL **9 HOURS**

The inspiration may be Italian but the taste is pure Southern comfort. Countertop cooking is in again, but today's slow cookers are plugged in to more sophisticated flavors— dinners worthy of weekend company.

1 (8-oz.) pkg. sliced fresh mushrooms	1 (8-oz.) can tomato sauce
1 large sweet onion, halved and sliced	3 Tbsp. tomato paste
1 (3- to 4-lb.) boneless chuck roast, trimmed	1 tsp. dried Italian seasoning
1 tsp. black pepper	2 Tbsp. cornstarch
2 Tbsp. olive oil	Chopped fresh oregano, for garnish (optional)
1 (1-oz.) envelope dry onion soup mix	Mashed potatoes, for serving
1 (14-oz.) can beef broth	

1. Place mushrooms and onion in a lightly greased 5- to 6-quart slow cooker.

2. Sprinkle roast with pepper. Heat oil in a large skillet over medium-high. Brown roast on all sides in hot oil.

3. Place roast on top of mushrooms and onion in slow cooker. Sprinkle onion soup mix over roast; pour beef broth and tomato sauce over roast. Cover and cook on LOW 8 to 10 hours or until meat shreds easily with a fork.

4. Transfer roast to a cutting board; cut into large chunks, removing any large pieces of fat. Keep roast warm.

5. Skim fat from juices in slow cooker; stir in tomato paste and Italian seasoning. Stir together cornstarch and 2 tablespoons water in a small bowl until smooth; add to juices in slow cooker, stirring until blended. Increase heat to HIGH. Cover and cook until mixture is thickened, about 40 minutes. Stir in roast. Garnish with fresh oregano, if desired. Serve with mashed potatoes.

Spiced Lamb with Roasted Grapes and Cranberries

SERVES **6**   ACTIVE **15 MIN.**

TOTAL **1 HOUR, 30 MIN., INCLUDING GRAPES AND CRANBERRIES**

Order trimmed lamb from your butcher a few days ahead.

3 (8-rib) lamb rib roasts (1½ lb. each), trimmed

1 Tbsp. red curry powder

1½ tsp. kosher salt

1½ tsp. black pepper

Roasted Grapes and Cranberries (recipe follows)

5 Tbsp. olive oil, divided

2 Tbsp. honey

Fresh rosemary sprigs, fresh bay leaves, and sliced clementines, for garnish (optional)

1. Preheat oven to 425°F. Sprinkle lamb on all sides with curry powder, salt, and pepper. Let stand 30 minutes.

2. Meanwhile, prepare Roasted Grapes and Cranberries as directed.

3. Heat 1 tablespoon oil in a 12-inch cast-iron skillet over medium. Brown lamb roasts on all sides in hot oil, 6 to 7 minutes. Place roasts, meat sides up, in skillet. Stir together honey and remaining 4 tablespoons oil; brush mixture on tops and sides of lamb.

4. Roast in preheated oven until a meat thermometer inserted into thickest portion registers 135°F (medium-rare), 15 to 18 minutes. Remove lamb from oven; let stand 10 minutes. Cut into chops, and serve with Roasted Grapes and Cranberries. Garnish with rosemary sprigs, bay leaves, and clementintes, if desired.

Roasted Grapes and Cranberries

6 to 8 seedless green or red grape clusters (about 1 lb.)

1 cup fresh cranberries

1 Tbsp. olive oil

1 tsp. chopped fresh rosemary

1. Preheat oven to 400°F. Place grape clusters on a 15- x 10-inch jelly-roll pan. Stir together cranberries, olive oil, and rosemary in a small bowl. Spoon mixture over grape clusters.

2. Bake in preheated oven until grapes begin to blister and cranberry skins begin to split, 15 to 18 minutes, shaking pan occasionally. Serve immediately, or let stand up to 4 hours.

ANGEL FOOD CAKE WITH
BALSAMIC STRAWBERRIES,
PAGE 148

Easy, Elegant Desserts

The perfect ending to any meal is a little something sweet. These festive recipes only look like they took hours to make. However, they come together in a flash thanks to grocery store conveniences and boldly flavored ingredients.

Angel Food Cake with Balsamic Strawberries

SERVES **8** ACTIVE **10 MIN.** TOTAL **25 MIN.**

Use a good-quality aged vinegar for the best flavor.

½ cup packed brown sugar	**8 (2-inch-thick) slices angel food cake**
¼ cup balsamic vinegar	**Whipped cream**
4 cups halved strawberries	**Fresh basil leaves, for garnish (optional)**

Combine sugar and vinegar in a large bowl; stir until sugar dissolves. Add berries; toss gently to coat. Let stand at room temperature 15 minutes, stirring occasionally. Spoon berries and sauce over cake slices. Top with whipped cream. Garnish with basil leaves, if desired.

Red Wine–Cherry Sundaes

SERVES **8** ACTIVE **10 MIN.** TOTAL **20 MIN.**

The wine tames the sweetness of the cherries while it simmers, leaving flavorful complexity (minus any alcohol) behind.

4 cups unsweetened frozen pitted dark sweet cherries, thawed	**2 tsp. fresh lemon juice**
2 cups dry red wine	**¼ tsp. kosher salt**
¼ cup brown sugar	**4 cups vanilla ice cream**
	Fresh basil leaves, for garnish (optional)

1. Combine cherries, wine, brown sugar, lemon juice, and salt in a saucepan; bring to a boil. Lightly crush about half of cherries with a potato masher. Reduce heat, and cook until reduced to about 2 cups.

2. Let stand 5 minutes. Spoon warm cherry sauce over ice cream. Garnish with basil leaves, if desired.

Wine-Poached Pears with Currants

SERVES **8**   ACTIVE **15 MIN.**   TOTAL **25 MIN.**

2 cups sweet white wine (such as Gewürztraminer)

1 cup water

¼ cup granulated sugar

2 Tbsp. fresh lemon juice

⅛ tsp. kosher salt

4 black peppercorns

2 (3-inch) cinnamon sticks

8 Bosc pears, peeled, halved lengthwise, and cored

2 cups fresh red currants

1. Combine wine, the water, sugar, lemon juice, salt, peppercorns, and cinnamon sticks in a large saucepan. Stir with a whisk. Add pears; cover and bring to a boil. Reduce heat, and simmer until pears are tender, about 9 minutes. Remove pears with a slotted spoon. Increase heat to high; bring cooking liquid to a boil. Cook until reduced to 1½ cups, about 5 minutes. Discard cinnamon and peppercorns.

2. Place 2 pear halves in each of 8 bowls; drizzle with about 3 tablespoons cooking liquid. Top each serving with ¼ cup currants.

Sparkling Raspberry Parfaits

SERVES **8**   ACTIVE **5 MIN.**   TOTAL **5 MIN.**

Raspberry sparkling wine has a pretty pink color and lightly sweet flavor; you can use regular sparkling wine for a less sweet dessert, or raspberry-flavored seltzer water instead.

4 cups raspberry sorbet

2 cups chilled raspberry sparkling wine (such as Verdi Raspberry Sparkletini)

¼ cup shaved bittersweet chocolate

Fresh mint leaves, for garnish (optional)

Scoop ½ cup sorbet into each of 8 wineglasses or small bowls; drizzle each serving with ¼ cup wine. Top each serving with 1½ teaspoons chocolate. Garnish with mint leaves, if desired. Serve immediately.

Spirited Sparklers

Is it sparkling wine or Champagne? True Champagne is produced in the French region of the same name.

Other delicious, sparkling varietals are available from producers around the globe.

Asti Sweet sparkling white wine made from Muscat grapes near the Italian Piedmont town of Asti. Serve chilled with fruit, pastries, and simple desserts.

California Sparkling Wine Hundreds of producers in the state make sparkling wine, from dry to sweet, using Chardonnay, Pinot Blanc, and Pinot Noir grapes.

Cava Dry to sweet white or rosé sparkling wine made in Spain from Parellada, Xarel-lo, or Macebeu grapes. Serve with crudité, cheese, creamy sauces, salads, and seafood.

Cremant Aged, sparkling French white and rosé wines made outside of Champagne from hand-picked grapes. Serve with omelets and rich foods, but also salads and pizza.

Franciacorta Dry to sweet sparkling white and red wines made from Chardonnay, Pinot Nero, and Pinot Bianco grapes in Lombardy, Italy. Serve with ravioli, truffles, tomato sauce, and pizza.

Lambrusco Both a red wine grape and type of red wine made in the Emilia-Romagna and Lombardy regions of Italy. From dry to sweet, lightly sparkling "frizzante" Lambrusco is the most prized. Serve with sausages, cured meats, barbecue, aged dry cheeses, pizza, and stone fruits.

Prosecco Light, sparkling white wine named for the Italian village of Prosecco, where it originated. It is traditionally made from Glera grapes, but other varieties may also be used. Serve with nuts, charcuterie, fried or salty foods, and seafood.

White Chocolate Panna Cotta

SERVES **6**   ACTIVE **15 MIN.**   TOTAL **8 HOURS 15 MIN.**

Panna cotta is a decadent Italian dessert that you can make in minutes, but it requires at least 8 hours to chill to dense, creamy perfection.

1 envelope unflavored gelatin

2 cups half-and-half, divided

3 oz. white chocolate, chopped

1 cup fat-free sweetened condensed milk

½ tsp. vanilla extract

Shaved dark and white chocolate, for garnish (optional)

Espresso powder, for garnish (optional)

1. Sprinkle gelatin over 1 cup half-and-half in a small saucepan; let stand 1 to 2 minutes. Cook, stirring constantly, over medium until gelatin dissolves, about 3 minutes; remove from heat. Add white chocolate, stirring until chocolate melts.

2. Gradually stir in remaining 1 cup half-and-half, the condensed milk, and vanilla. Pour ½ cup custard into each of 6 (6-ounce) custard cups. Cover and chill 8 hours or until ready to serve. Turn out onto individual serving dishes. Top with shaved chocolate and a sprinkle of espresso powder, if desired.

White Chocolate 101

At its essence, white chocolate is a simple combo of cocoa butter and dairy milk. However, sugar, vanilla, and stabilizers are often added. According to the FDA, to legally be called "white chocolate," it must contain at least 20% cocoa butter, 3.5% milk fat, and a minimum of 14% total milk solids. In addition, it cannot have more than 55% carbohydrate sweeteners like sugar. The remaining percentage might be extracts or other flavorings or add-ins.

SUGARED
ICEBOX COOKIES,
PAGE 162

JOY
TO Parker

Christmas Cookies

No holiday would be complete without a plate of cookies for Santa and a cookie tin or two for family, friends, and colleagues. So we've made it easy to make an array of cookies using one base recipe.

Base Cookie Dough

MAKES **1½ TO 3 DOZEN**   ACTIVE **10 MIN.**
TOTAL **2 HOURS, 10 MIN.**

From slice-and-bake cookies to bars, cups, and sandwiches, the secret to bountiful batches of holiday cookies lies in this versatile buttery sugar cookie dough. Whip it up in mere minutes, and then flavor it, shape it, top it, or fill it multiple ways for a festive lineup of from-scratch goodies to enjoy and share.

¾ **cup unsalted butter, softened**

1¾ **cups granulated sugar**

¾ **tsp. kosher salt**

2 large eggs

1 tsp. vanilla extract

2½ **cups all-purpose flour**

1 tsp. baking powder

1. Beat butter, sugar, and salt with a heavy-duty stand mixer on medium-high until light and fluffy, about 3 minutes. Add eggs and vanilla. Beat on medium until combined, stopping to scrape down sides of bowl as needed.

2. With mixer running on low, add flour and baking powder to butter mixture, beating until just incorporated.

3. Shape dough into a disk, wrap tightly in plastic wrap, and chill until firm, at least 2 hours. Dough will keep in refrigerator, tightly wrapped, up to 2 weeks, or in freezer up to 3 months.

Variations

Chocolate Cookie Dough:
Use 2 cups all-purpose flour and ½ cup unsweetened dark cocoa powder in Step 2.

Orange- or Lemon-Scented Cookie Dough:
Whisk 1 Tbsp. grated lemon or orange zest (or a combination) into flour in Step 2 before adding it to butter mixture.

Cinnamon or Spice Cookie Dough:
Whisk 1 Tbsp. ground cinnamon or pumpkin pie spice into flour in Step 2 before adding it to butter mixture.

Gingerbread Cookie Dough:
Use 1½ cups granulated sugar and ¼ cup unsulphured molasses in Step 1. Whisk 1½ Tbsp. ground ginger into flour in Step 2 before adding it to butter mixture.

SUGARED
ICEBOX COOKIES,
PAGE 162

GOLDEN CITRUS STARS,
PAGE 162
THUMBPRINT COOKIES,
PAGE 164
FROSTED CINNAMON
BAR COOKIES, PAGE 163

George

CARAMEL
COOKIE CUPS,
PAGE 167

Sugared Icebox Cookies

MAKES **ABOUT 3 DOZEN**   ACTIVE **20 MIN.**
TOTAL **3 HOURS, 35 MIN.**

You can embellish these slice-and-bake cookies with other ingredients, such as chopped nuts, toasted coconut, or candy sprinkles.

Base Cookie Dough (page 158)

2 cups white chocolate chips

2 tablespoons shortening

Red and green sanding sugar

1. Prepare Base Cookie Dough as directed through Step 2.

2. Shape shape dough into 2 (8-inch) logs. Wrap each log with plastic wrap; chill until firm, at least 3 hours or up to 2 days.

3. Preheat oven to 350°F. Slice logs into ¼-inch-thick rounds. Place slices 1 inch apart on baking sheets lined with parchment paper. Bake at 350°F until edges of slices are golden, 10 to 12 minutes. Transfer cookies to wire racks, and cool completely, about 20 minutes.

4. Place white chocolate chips and shortening in a medium microwave-safe bowl and heat in microwave on 50% power in 20 second intervals, stirring well between intervals until melted and smooth. Dip half of each cookie in melted white chocolate mixture, then run bottom of cookie slightly along edge of bowl to remove excess. Return to parchment paper and immediately sprinkle with red and green sanding sugar. Allow to set at room temperature.

Golden Citrus Stars

MAKES **ABOUT 2 DOZEN**   ACTIVE **35 MIN.**
TOTAL **3 HOURS, 45 MIN.**

Lemon-Scented Base Cookie Dough (page 158)

3 cups powdered sugar

1½ Tbsp. meringue powder

¾ tsp. lemon extract

Yellow or metallic gold food coloring gel

Candy sprinkles

Nonpareils

1. Prepare Lemon-Scented variation of Base Cookie Dough as directed.

2. Preheat oven to 350°F. Roll chilled dough to ¼-inch thickness on a lightly floured surface. Cut with desired star-shape cutters, rerolling scraps as needed. (If dough becomes warm and sticky, place in refrigerator for 15 minutes.)

3. Place cookies 2 inches apart on 2 parchment paper-lined baking sheets; chill 20 minutes. Bake in preheated oven until tops of cookies are dry to touch, about 10 minutes. Cool on baking sheets 2 minutes. Transfer to a wire rack to cool completely, about 30 minutes.

4. Meanwhile, beat powdered sugar, ¼ cup warm water, and the meringue powder with a heavy-duty electric stand mixer on medium speed until smooth and glossy, about 2 minutes. Add lemon extract; beat until combined, adding up to 2 tablespoons water, 1 teaspoon at a time, until desired consistency is reached. Divide frosting between 2 small bowls. Tint 1 bowl with desired amount of yellow or metallic gold food coloring gel. Leave remaining bowl of icing untinted.

5. Decorate cookies with icing, candy sprinkles, and nonpareils as desired. Let dry completely, about 1 hour.

Frosted Cinnamon Bar Cookies

MAKES **1½ DOZEN** ACTIVE **30 MIN.**
TOTAL **3 HOURS, 55 MIN.**

Cinnamon Base Cookie Dough (page 158)

¼ cup unsalted butter, softened

2 oz. cream cheese, softened

2 cups powdered sugar

1 Tbsp. heavy whipping cream

¼ tsp. vanilla extract

Hot cinnamon-flavor candies

Nonpareils

1. Prepare Cinnamon variation of Base Cookie Dough as directed.

2. Preheat oven to 350°F. Lightly grease an 8-inch square baking pan with cooking spray. Line bottom and sides of pan with parchment paper, allowing 2 to 3 inches to extend over 2 sides.

3. Press chilled dough into an even layer in prepared pan. Bake in preheated oven until dry to touch, about 22 minutes. Cool completely in pan on a wire rack, about 1 hour. Lift baked cookie dough from pan using parchment paper as handles; place on a cutting board.

4. Beat butter and cream cheese with a heavy-duty electric stand mixer on medium until creamy, about 2 minutes. Reduce speed to low; with mixer running, gradually add powdered sugar, beating until smooth. Add cream and vanilla; beat on medium-high until blended, about 20 seconds.

5. Spread frosting on baked cookies; cut into 18 squares, bars, or triangles. Sprinkle with candies and nonpareils.

Gingerbread Cutouts

MAKES **ABOUT 2 DOZEN** ACTIVE **35 MIN.**
TOTAL **3 HOURS, 45 MIN.**

Gingerbread Base Cookie Dough (page 158)

3 cups powdered sugar

1½ Tbsp. meringue powder

¾ tsp. vanilla extract

Red and green food coloring gel

Candy sprinkles

Nonpareils

1. Prepare Gingerbread variation of Base Cookie Dough as directed.

2. Preheat oven to 350°F. Roll chilled dough to ¼-inch thickness on a lightly floured surface. Cut with desired-shape cutters, rerolling scraps as needed. (If dough becomes warm and sticky, place in refrigerator for 15 minutes.)

3. Place cookies 2 inches apart on 2 parchment paper-lined baking sheets; chill 20 minutes. Bake in preheated oven until tops of cookies are dry to touch, about 10 minutes. Cool on baking sheets 2 minutes. Transfer to a wire rack to cool completely, about 30 minutes.

4. Meanwhile, beat powdered sugar, ¼ cup warm water, and the meringue powder with a heavy-duty electric stand mixer on medium speed until smooth and glossy, about 2 minutes. Add vanilla; beat until combined, adding up to 2 tablespoons water, 1 teaspoon at a time, until desired consistency is reached. Divide icing among 3 small bowls. Tint 1 bowl with desired amount of red food coloring gel. Tint second bowl with desired amount of green food coloring gel. Leave remaining bowl of icing untinted.

5. Decorate cookies with icing, candy sprinkles, and nonpareils as desired. Let dry completely, about 1 hour.

Thumbprint Cookies

MAKES **2 DOZEN**   ACTIVE **30 MIN.**
TOTAL **3 HOURS, 5 MIN.**

**Base Cookie Dough
(page 158)**

**Fruit jam or jelly,
chocolate chunks,
or nut halves**

1. Prepare Base Cookie Dough as directed through Step 2. Cover dough in mixing bowl with plastic and chill until firm, at least 2 hours.

2. Preheat oven to 350°F. Drop dough by heaping tablespoons 2 inches apart on 2 parchment paper-lined baking sheets. Use a ¼-teaspoon measure to gently press a hollow in center of each dough mound. Fill each hollow with ½ teaspoon jam or jelly, a chocolate chunk, or a nut half. Chill 20 minutes.

3. Bake in preheated oven until cookies are pale golden, 13 to 15 minutes, rotating baking sheets halfway through.

S'more Cookies

MAKES **2 DOZEN**   ACTIVE **30 MIN.**
TOTAL **2 HOURS, 45 MIN.**

**Chocolate Base Cookie
Dough (page 158)**

**¼ cup crushed graham
crackers**

**12 large marshmallows,
cut in half**

1. Prepare Chocolate variation of Base Cookie Dough as directed.

2. Preheat oven to 350°F. Roll chilled dough to ¼-inch thickness on a lightly floured surface. Cut with a round cutter, rerolling scraps as needed. (If dough becomes warm and sticky, place in refrigerator for 15 minutes.)

3. Place cookies 2 inches apart on 2 parchment paper-lined baking sheets; chill 20 minutes. Bake in preheated oven until cookies are almost set, about 8 minutes. Remove from oven.

4. Increase heat to high broil, with oven rack 4 inches from heat. Top each cookie with 1 marshmallow half, cut side down. Broil until marshmallows are lightly browned, 1 to 2 minutes. Sprinkle cookies with graham cracker crumbs. Cool cookies on baking sheets 2 minutes; transfer to a wire rack.

Caramel Cookie Cups

MAKES **3 DOZEN**   ACTIVE **45 MIN.**

TOTAL **3 HOURS, 50 MIN.**

Orange-Scented or Spiced Base Cookie Dough (page 158)

½ cup unsalted butter, softened

4 oz. cream cheese, softened

2 Tbsp. jarred caramel sauce or topping, plus more for drizzling

2½ cups powdered sugar

¼ tsp. orange extract

½ tsp. flaky sea salt, plus more for sprinkling

40 toasted pecan halves

1. Prepare Orange-Scented or Spiced variation of Base Cookie Dough as directed.

2. Divide dough into 40 (1-tablespoon) balls (about ½ ounce each). Place 1 ball in each cup of 2 (24-cup) lightly greased miniature muffin pans. (You'll fill only 40 cups.) Using a teaspoon measure, press dough into bottom and up sides of muffin cups. Chill 20 minutes.

3. Preheat oven to 350°F. Bake in preheated oven until cookies are dry to touch and shape is set, about 10 minutes. Immediately press cookies again with teaspoon. Cool cookie cups in pans on a wire rack 5 minutes. Transfer cookie cups to wire rack to cool completely, about 30 minutes.

4. Meanwhile, beat butter, cream cheese, and caramel sauce in the bowl of a heavy-duty electric stand mixer on medium speed until creamy, 1 to 2 minutes. Reduce speed to low; with mixer running, gradually add powdered sugar, beating until smooth. Beat in vanilla extract and flaky salt. Transfer filling to a piping bag fitted with a large star tip, and evenly pipe into cooled cookie cups. Drizzle about 1 teaspoon caramel sauce on each filled cookie cup. Sprinkle each cookie with desired amount of flaky sea salt, and top each with a toasted pecan half.

"You're just as likely to have a ladder in your kitchen as you are in the garage, so reach for what's easy and achievable. The goal is to create something warm and welcoming, and a few lights, garland, and ornaments can take a triangular ladder from everyday function to holiday folly."

—MINDI SHAPIRO LEVINE

Thanks to These Vendors

We wish to thank the following vendors and resources whose products were photographed on the pages of this book.

Accent Décor	Etsy	New Arcadia Studio	Wayfair
Anna Weatherley Designs	Hobby Lobby	OKA	Wedgwood
Anthropologie	HomArt	Osborne & Little	Z Gallerie
At Home	Home Goods	Park Hill Collection	
Cody Foster	Lion Ribbon	Royal Crown Derby	
Ebay	McCoy Pottery	Target	

Special thanks to these local businesses, shops, artisans, and restaurants.

A'mano	Circa	Katherine B. Melvin Design	Paige Albright Orientals
ALKMY	Davis Wholesale Florist	Laura Deems, artist	Patina
Brick & Tin	Goodwill	Leaf & Petal	Post Office Pies
Bromberg's	Greenhouse	Oak Street Garden Shop	Shoppe
Buffy Hargett Flowers	Hammett		Surin of Thailand

Thanks to the following individuals and venues for allowing us to photograph their spaces.

The Cobbs Family

The Hargett-Miller Family

The Morton Family

The Varner Family

General Index

A

A Natural Noël, 38–47
activities, record of, 190
agave spirits, 72
All-Star Accents, 26–37
amaryllis, 32–33
antiques, decorating with, 41
"App-y" New Year!, 94–103

B

Beatty, Lindsey, 14–25
Bedrooms
  child, 46–47
  master, 24–25
Beverage tips
  agave spirits, 72
  Southern liqueurs, 103
  sparkling wines, 152

C

Candles
  Anthropologie candlesticks, 16–17
  soda can votive holder, 50
casserole toppings, 88
Checklists
  Christmas cards, 189
  decorating, 182
  gifts, 188
  thank-you notes, 192
child's room, decorating, 46–47
Christmas 2024, notes for, 192
Christmas card list, 189
Christmas Cookies, 156–167
Christmas dinner planner, 186–187

Christmas tree(s)
  caring for fresh, 183
  flocked, 22
  ladder tree, 168
  mini tree, 25
  ribbon decorations for, 20–21
  selecting fresh, 183
  silver-tipped fir, 20–21
Cocktail bars
  bar nook, 44
  Champagne station, 22
  dining room console, 18–19
Cramer, Floyd, 45

D

December calendar, 180–181
decorating planner, 182
decorating toolkit, 182
dressmaker's form, decorating a, 52–53

E

Easy, Elegant Desserts, 146–155
eggnog, 22

F

Fireplace decorations
  evergreen garland, 21
  ornament-filled lanterns, 21
Floral arrangements
  amaryllis, 32–33
  caring for, 42
  large centerpiece, 36–37
  paperwhites, 30–31
  succulents and moss, 34–35
  tips for, 30

Food tips
  casserole toppings, 88
  oysters, 115
  soup garnishes, 111
  trussing poultry, 136
  white chocolate, 155
  winter greens, 123
foyer, floral arrangements for, 30–31

G

Garland
  as centerpiece, 16–17
  evergreen and eucalyptus, 21
  faux fur stole, 50–51
  staircase, 40–41
gift list, 188
Greenery
  evergreen and eucalyptus garland, 21
  evergreen wreath, 28–29
  on mirrors and pictures, 40–41

H

Hargett, Buffy, 26–37
Hark, the Sorbet Colors Sing!, 14–25
Ho Ho Hoedown, 70–79
Holiday Planner, 177–192
Homecoming Feast, 80–93
hotlines, holiday, 179

K

kitchen decorating, 22–23

L

Levine, Mindi Shapiro, 48–55, 168

M

Main Attractions, 134–146
master bedroom, decorating, 24–25
memories, record of, 190–191
Menus
    "App-y" New Year, 95
    Ho Ho Hoedown, 71
    Homecoming Feast, 81
    Merry Brunchmas, 59
Merry Brunchmas, 58–69
Merry Remix, 48–55
metric equivalents, 172
mirror decorations, 25

N

November calendar, 178–179

O

Ornaments
    Bubble Glass, 22–23
    copper and gold, 42–43
    Shiny Brite, 21
    as tabletop decorations, 36–37

Outdoor decorating
    evergreen wreath for front door, 28–29
    hanging wall tree, 54–55
    metal decorations, 54–55
    repeating elements, 6–7
oysters, 115

P

paperwhites, 30–31
party planner, 184–185
piano, 43, 45
Planners
    Christmas dinner, 186–187
    decorating, 182
    party, 184–185
poultry, trussing, 136

R

recipes, list of favorite, 191

S

Seasonal Starters, 106–115
soda can Christmas tree, 54
soda can votive holder, 50
soup garnishes, 111
Southern liqueurs, 103
sparkling wines, 152
Starches & Grains, 126–133
Stylists
    Beatty, Lindsey, 14–25
    Hargett, Buffy, 26–37
    Levine, Mindi Shapiro, 48–55, 168
    Varner, Kathleen, 38–47
succulents and moss floral arrangement, 34–35

T

Tablescapes
    layered place settings, 18, 45
    mixing plates, 45
    personal style, 16–18
    succulent and moss floral arrangement, 34–35
thank-you notes, record of, 192
tinsel, 42–43
traditions, record of, 190

V

Varner, Kathleen, 38–47
vendors, list of, 169
visits and visitors, record of, 191

W

white chocolate, 155
winter greens, 123
Winter Vegetables, 116–125
Wreaths
    in bedroom, 24–25
    evergreen, making an, 28–29
    necktie, 50
    window, 47

Metric Charts

The recipes that appear in this cookbook use the standard US method for measuring liquid and dry or solid ingredients (teaspoons, tablespoons, and cups). The information on these pages is provided to help cooks outside the United States successfully use these recipes. All equivalents are approximate.

Metric Equivalents for Different Types of Ingredients

A standard cup measure of a dry or solid ingredient will vary in weight depending on the type of ingredient. A standard cup of liquid is the same volume for any type of liquid. Use the following chart when converting standard cup measures to grams (weight) or milliliters (volume).

STANDARD CUP	FINE POWDER (ex. flour)	GRAIN (ex. rice)	GRANULAR (ex. sugar)	LIQUID SOLIDS (ex. butter)	LIQUID (ex. milk)
1	140 g	150 g	190 g	200 g	240 ml
3/4	105 g	113 g	143 g	150 g	180 ml
2/3	93 g	100 g	125 g	133 g	160 ml
1/2	70 g	75 g	95 g	100 g	120 ml
1/3	47 g	50 g	63 g	67 g	80 ml
1/4	35 g	38 g	48 g	50 g	60 ml
1/8	18 g	19 g	24 g	25 g	30 ml

Useful Equivalents for Liquid Ingredients by Volume

TSP	TBSP	CUPS	FL OZ	ML	L
1/4 tsp				1 ml	
1/2 tsp				2 ml	
1 tsp				5 ml	
3 tsp	1 Tbsp		1/2 fl oz	15 ml	
	2 Tbsp	1/8 cup	1 fl oz	30 ml	
	4 Tbsp	1/4 cup	2 fl oz	60 ml	
	5 1/3 Tbsp	1/3 cup	3 fl oz	80 ml	
	8 Tbsp	1/2 cup	4 fl oz	120 ml	
	10 2/3 Tbsp	2/3 cup	5 fl oz	160 ml	
	12 Tbsp	3/4 cup	6 fl oz	180 ml	
	16 Tbsp	1 cup	8 fl oz	240 ml	
	1 pt	2 cups	16 fl oz	480 ml	
	1 qt	4 cups	32 fl oz	960 ml	
			33 fl oz	1000 ml	1 L

Useful Equivalents for Dry Ingredients by Weight

(To convert ounces to grams, multiply the number of ounces by 30.)

OZ	LB	G
1 oz	1/16 lb	30 g
4 oz	1/4 lb	120 g
8 oz	1/2 lb	240 g
12 oz	3/4 lb	360 g
16 oz	1 lb	480 g

Useful Equivalents for Length

(To convert inches to centimeters, multiply the number of inches by 2.5.)

IN	FT	YD	CM	M
1 in			2.5 cm	
6 in	1/2 ft		15 cm	
12 in	1 ft		30 cm	
36 in	3 ft	1 yd	90 cm	
40 in			100 cm	1 m

Useful Equivalents for Cooking/Oven Temperatures

	FAHRENHEIT	CELSIUS	GAS MARK
FREEZE WATER	32°F	0°C	
ROOM TEMPERATURE	68°F	20°C	
BOIL WATER	212°F	100°C	
BAKE	325°F	160°C	3
	350°F	180°C	4
	375°F	190°C	5
	400°F	200°C	6
	425°F	220°C	7
	450°F	230°C	8
BROIL			Grill

Recipe Index

A

Almond(s)
Honey-Roasted Brussels Sprouts, 123
Nutty Granola with Whipped Ricotta
    and Berries, 63
Andouille Mac-n-Cheese, 128
Angel Food Cake with Balsamic
    Strawberries, 148
Appetizers. See also Starters
Apricot-Gorgonzola Bites, 101
Bacon-Bourbon Fig Bites, 82
Feta Fondue, 100
Jalapeño Popper Dip, 73
Pig Pinwheels, 96
Prosciutto-Asparagus Wraps, 101
Relish Tray Skewers, 100
Shrimp Cocktail with Five-Ingredient
    Cocktail Sauce, 100
Smoky Potato Skin Bites, 73
Apples
Apple-Cabbage Slaw, 76
Beet and Carrot Soup, 108
Wild Rice with Apples, 132
Apricot-Gorgonzola Bites, 101
Artichokes
Relish Tray Skewers, 100
Asparagus-Prosciutto Wraps, 101
Avocados Stuffed with Crab, 114

B

Bacon
Bacon-Bourbon Fig Bites, 82
Endive and Cress Salad with Bacon-
    Cider Dressing, 108
Green Beans with Bacon and
    Breadcrumbs, 125
Jalapeño Popper Dip, 73
Smoky Pepper-Pecan Sugared
    Bacon, 60
Smoky Potato Skin Bites, 73
Wild Rice with Bacon and Fennel, 89
Base Cookie Dough, 158
Beans
Green Beans with Bacon and
    Breadcrumbs, 125
Shrimp Cakes with Roasted Garlic
    Sauce, 114
Beef
Beef Tenderloin with Onion
    Confit, 142
Bourbon and Cherry Glazed
    Brisket, 76
Italian Pot Roast, 142
Beet and Carrot Soup, 108

Beverages
Blushing Paloma Punch, 72
Champagne Cocktail with Sparkling
    Cranberries, 96
Cheery Pitcher Cheladas, 60
Ruby Negroni, 82
Southern-Style Affogato, 103
Blue cheese
Apricot-Gorgonzola Bites, 101
Bacon-Bourbon Fig Bites, 82
Endive and Cress Salad with Bacon-
    Cider Dressing, 108
Blushing Paloma Punch, 72
Bourbon and Cherry Glazed Brisket, 76
Brunch recipes
Cheery Pitcher Cheladas, 60
Nutty Granola with Whipped Ricotta
    and Berries, 63
Smoky Pepper-Pecan Sugared
    Bacon, 60
Spiced Cranberry-Pecan Rolls, 69
Spinach-Feta Quiche with Sweet
    Potato Crust, 64
Brussels Sprouts, Honey-Roasted, 123
Butter, Rosemary-Maple, 77
Butternut Soup, Curried, 111

C

Cabbage-Apple Slaw, 76
Cajun Étoufée, 136
Cakes
Angel Food Cake with Balsamic
    Strawberries, 148
Chocolate-Toffee-Gingerbread
    Cake, 91
Caramel Cookie Cups, 167
Caramel Thumbprint Tartlets, 78
Carrots
Beet and Carrot Soup, 108
Carrot Orzo, 133
Roasted Rainbow Carrots with Carrot
    Top-Herb Gremolata, 123
Cauliflower with Garlic-Anchovy
    Sauce, Roasted Romanesco
    and, 118
Celery and Herb Salad with
    Pomegranate Seeds, 111
Champagne Cocktail with Sparkling
    Cranberries, 96
Cheery Pitcher Cheladas, 60
**Cheese. See also Blue cheese; Cream
    cheese; Feta; Goat cheese;
    Parmesan**
Andouille Mac-n-Cheese, 128
Crusty Spinach Casserole, 88
Jalapeño Popper Dip, 73
Nutty Granola with Whipped Ricotta
    and Berries, 63
Smoky Potato Skin Bites, 73
Sweet Potato Stacks, 128

Cherries
Bourbon and Cherry Glazed
    Brisket, 76
Honey-Roasted Brussels Sprouts, 123
Red Wine-Cherry Sundaes, 148
Chile peppers
Jalapeño Popper Dip, 73
Relish Tray Skewers, 100
Sweet Potato Soup with Fried Sage
    Leaves, 84
Chocolate
Chocolate Cookie Dough, 158
Chocolate-Toffee-Gingerbread
    Cake, 91
Silky Ganache, 92
S'more Cookies, 164
Sparkling Raspberry Parfaits, 152
White Chocolate Panna Cotta, 155
Cinnamon or Spice Cookie Dough, 158
Cookies
Base Cookie Dough, 158
Caramel Cookie Cups, 167
Caramel Thumbprint Tartlets, 78
Chocolate Cookie Dough, 158
Cinnamon or Spice Cookie
    Dough, 158
Frosted Cinnamon Bar Cookies, 163
Gingerbread Cookie Dough, 158
Gingerbread Cutouts, 163
Golden Citrus Stars, 162
Orange- or Lemon-Scented Cookie
    Dough, 158
S'more Cookies, 164
Spiced Sorghum Cookies, 92
Sugared Icebox Cookies, 162
Thumbprint Cookies, 164
Cornish Game Hens, 136
Crab, Avocados Stuffed with, 114
Cranberries
Champagne Cocktail with Sparkling
    Cranberries, 96
Roasted Grapes and Cranberries, 144
Sparkling Cranberries, 96
Spiced Cranberry-Pecan Rolls, 69
Spiced Lamb with Roasted Grapes
    and Cranberries, 144
Cream cheese
Caramel Cookie Cups, 167
Cream Cheese Pastry Shells, 78
Crusty Spinach Casserole, 88
Frosted Cinnamon Bar Cookies, 163
Jalapeño Popper Dip, 73
Crusty Spinach Casserole, 88
Currants, Wine-Poached Pears
    with, 151
Curried Butternut Soup, 111

D

Desserts. See also Cookies
Angel Food Cake with Balsamic
Strawberries, 148
Chocolate-Toffee-Gingerbread
Cake, 91
Red Wine-Cherry Sundaes, 148
Sparkling Raspberry Parfaits, 152
White Chocolate Panna Cotta, 155
Wine-Poached Pears with
Currants, 151

E

Endive and Cress Salad with Bacon-
Cider Dressing, 108
Étoufée, Cajun, 136

F

Fennel, Wild Rice with Bacon and, 89
Feta
Feta Fondue, 100
Spinach-Feta Quiche with Sweet
Potato Crust, 64
Fig Bites, Bacon-Bourbon, 82
Fried Sage Leaves, 84
Frosted Cinnamon Bar Cookies, 163
Frostings and icings
Royal Icing, 92
Silky Ganache, 92

G

Garlic
Garlic-Butter Breadcrumbs, 115
Roasted Romanesco and Cauliflower
with Garlic-Anchovy Sauce, 118
Shrimp Cakes with Roasted Garlic
Sauce, 114
Ginger Whipped Cream, 91
Gingerbread Cookie Dough, 158
Gingerbread Cutouts, 163
Goat cheese
Mesclun, Pear, and Goat Cheese
Salad, 84
Prosciutto-Asparagus Wraps, 101
Golden Citrus Stars, 162
Grains and pasta. See also Grits
Carrot Orzo, 133
Nutty Granola with Whipped Ricotta
and Berries, 63
Pecan-Corn Muffins, 77
Quinoa with Toasted Pecans, 132
Shrimp Cakes with Roasted Garlic
Sauce, 114
Grapefruit
Blushing Paloma Punch, 72
Grapes
Roasted Grapes and Cranberries, 144
Spiced Lamb with Roasted Grapes
and Cranberries, 144
Green Beans with Bacon and
Breadcrumbs, 125

Greens
Apple-Cabbage Slaw, 76
Avocados Stuffed with Crab, 114
Mesclun, Pear, and Goat Cheese
Salad, 84
Shrimp Cakes with Roasted Garlic
Sauce, 114
Grillades and Grits, 139
Grits
Grillades and Grits, 139
Ham Hock Grits, 139

H

Ham Hock Grits, 139
Honey-Roasted Brussels Sprouts, 123
Horseradish Sauce, 142

I

Italian Pot Roast, 142

J

Jalapeño Popper Dip, 73

L

Lamb with Roasted Grapes and
Cranberries, Spiced, 144
Lemon(s)
Golden Citrus Stars, 162
Orange- or Lemon-Scented Cookie
Dough, 158

M

Make-Ahead Yeast Rolls, 83
Mango(es)
Cheery Pitcher Cheladas, 60
Mashed Potatoes and Parsnips, 118
Mesclun, Pear, and Goat Cheese
Salad, 84
Muffins, Pecan-Corn, 77
Mushrooms
Italian Pot Roast, 142
Mushroom Carpaccio with Gremolata
and Shaved Parmigiano, 122

N

Nutty Granola with Whipped Ricotta
and Berries, 63

O

Okra
Relish Tray Skewers, 100
Onions
Beef Tenderloin with Onion
Confit, 142
Jalapeño Popper Dip, 73
Pork Roast with Vidalia-Pepita
Relish, 89
Orange(s)
Caramel Cookie Cups, 167
Cornish Game Hens, 136
Orange- or Lemon-Scented Cookie
Dough, 158
Oysters Two Ways, 115

P

Pancetta and Pine Nuts, Roasted
Radicchio with, 122
Parmesan
Andouille Mac-n-Cheese, 128
Carrot Orzo, 133
Mushroom Carpaccio with Gremolata
and Shaved Parmigiano, 122
Spinach-Feta Quiche with Sweet
Potato Crust, 64
Sweet Potato Stacks, 128
Parsnips and Potatoes, Mashed, 118
Pastry Shells, Cream Cheese, 78
Pears
Mesclun, Pear, and Goat Cheese
Salad, 84
Wine-Poached Pears with
Currants, 151
Pecans
Apricot-Gorgonzola Bites, 101
Bacon-Bourbon Fig Bites, 82
Caramel Cookie Cups, 167
Pecan-Corn Muffins, 77
Quinoa with Toasted Pecans, 132
Smoky Pepper-Pecan Sugared
Bacon, 60
Spiced Cranberry-Pecan Rolls, 69
Wild Rice with Apples, 132
Pepita-Vidalia Relish, Pork Roast
with, 89
Pig Pinwheels, 96
Pine Nuts and Pancetta, Roasted
Radicchio with, 122
Pink Peppercorn Mignonette, 115
Pistachios
Nutty Granola with Whipped Ricotta
and Berries, 63
Pistachio-Pomegranate Rice, 133
Pomegranate
Celery and Herb Salad with
Pomegranate Seeds, 111
Pistachio-Pomegranate Rice, 133
Ruby Negroni, 82
Pork. See also Bacon
Grillades and Grits, 139
Ham Hock Grits, 139
Pork Roast with Vidalia-Pepita
Relish, 89
Prosciutto-Asparagus Wraps, 101
Roasted Radicchio with Pancetta and
Pine Nuts, 122
Potatoes. See also Sweet potatoes
Italian Pot Roast, 142
Mashed Potatoes and Parsnips, 118
Smoky Potato Skin Bites, 73
Prosciutto-Asparagus Wraps, 101

Q

Quiche with Sweet Potato Crust,
Spinach-Feta, 64
Quinoa with Toasted Pecans, 132

174

R

Radicchio
  Endive and Cress Salad with Bacon-
    Cider Dressing, 108
  Roasted Radicchio with Pancetta and
    Pine Nuts, 122
Raspberry(ies)
  Nutty Granola with Whipped Ricotta
    and Berries, 63
  Sparkling Raspberry Parfaits, 152
Red Wine-Cherry Sundaes, 148
Relish Tray Skewers, 100
Rice
  Cajun Étoufée, 136
  Pistachio-Pomegranate Rice, 133
  Wild Rice with Apples, 132
  Wild Rice with Bacon and Fennel, 89
  Roasted Grapes and Cranberries, 144
Roasted Radicchio with Pancetta and
    Pine Nuts, 122
Roasted Rainbow Carrots with Carrot
    Top-Herb Gremolata, 123
Roasted Romanesco and Cauliflower
    with Garlic-Anchovy Sauce, 118
Rolls
  Make-Ahead Yeast Rolls, 83
  Sage-Brown Butter Rolls, 109
  Spiced Cranberry-Pecan Rolls, 69
Romanesco and Cauliflower with
    Garlic-Anchovy Sauce,
    Roasted, 118
Rosemary-Maple Butter, 77
Royal Icing, 92
Ruby Negroni, 82

S

Sage-Brown Butter Rolls, 109
Salads
  Apple-Cabbage Slaw, 76
  Celery and Herb Salad with
    Pomegranate Seeds, 111
  Endive and Cress Salad with Bacon-
    Cider Dressing, 108
  Mesclun, Pear, and Goat Cheese
    Salad, 84
  Mushroom Carpaccio with Gremolata
    and Shaved Parmigiano, 122
Sauces
  Horseradish Sauce, 142
  Pink Peppercorn Mignonette, 115
Sausages
  Andouille Mac-n-Cheese, 128
  Pig Pinwheels, 96
Shellfish. See also Shrimp
  Avocados Stuffed with Crab, 114
  Cajun Étoufée, 136
  Oysters Two Ways, 115
Shrimp
  Shrimp Cakes with Roasted Garlic
    Sauce, 114
  Shrimp Cocktail with Five-Ingredient
    Cocktail Sauce, 100
Silky Ganache, 92
Slow cooker recipes
  Bourbon and Cherry Glazed
    Brisket, 76
  Italian Pot Roast, 142

Smoky Pepper-Pecan Sugared
    Bacon, 60
Smoky Potato Skin Bites, 73
S'more Cookies, 164
Soups
  Beet and Carrot Soup, 108
  Curried Butternut Soup, 111
  Sweet Potato Soup with Fried Sage
    Leaves, 84
Southern-Style Affogato, 103
Sparkling Cranberries, 96
Sparkling Raspberry Parfaits, 152
Spice or Cinnamon Cookie Dough, 158
Spiced Cranberry-Pecan Rolls, 69
Spiced Lamb with Roasted Grapes and
    Cranberries, 144
Spiced Sorghum Cookies, 92
Spinach
  Crusty Spinach Casserole, 88
  Spinach-Feta Quiche with Sweet
    Potato Crust, 64
Starters. See also Appetizers
  Avocados Stuffed with Crab, 114
  Beet and Carrot Soup, 108
  Celery and Herb Salad with
    Pomegranate Seeds, 111
  Curried Butternut Soup, 111
  Endive and Cress Salad with Bacon-
    Cider Dressing, 108
  Oysters Two Ways, 115
  Sage-Brown Butter Rolls, 109
  Shrimp Cakes with Roasted Garlic
    Sauce, 114
Strawberries, Angel Food Cake with
    Balsamic, 148
Sugared Icebox Cookies, 162
Sweet potatoes
  Spinach-Feta Quiche with Sweet
    Potato Crust, 64
  Sweet Potato Soup with Fried Sage
    Leaves, 84
  Sweet Potato Stacks, 128

T

Thumbprint Cookies, 164
Tomatoes
  Grillades and Grits, 139
  Relish Tray Skewers, 100

W

Walnuts
  Beet and Carrot Soup, 108
  Mesclun, Pear, and Goat Cheese
    Salad, 84
Wild Rice with Bacon and Fennel, 89
White Chocolate Panna Cotta, 155
Wild Rice with Apples, 132
Wild Rice with Bacon and Fennel, 89
Wine-Poached Pears with Currants, 151

DOTDASH MEREDITH CONSUMER MARKETING
Director, Direct Marketing-Books: Daniel Fagan
Marketing Operations Manager: Max Daily
Assistant Marketing Manager: Kylie Dazzo
Content Manager: Julie Doll
Marketing Coordinator: Elizabeth Moore
Senior Production Manager: Liza Ward

PRODUCED BY:
BLUELINE CREATIVE GROUP LLC
visit: bluelinecreativegroup.com
Executive Producer/Editor: Katherine Cobbs
Book Designer: Claire Cormany
Location Photographer: Laurey W. Glenn
Location Stylists: Lindsey Ellis Beatty, Buffy Hargett Miller, Mindi Shapiro-Levine, Kathleen Varner

STUDIO RECIPE PHOTOGRAPHY:
DOTDASH MEREDITH FOOD STUDIOS
Director: Allison Lowery
Photography Director: Sheri Wilson
Photo Editor: Catherine Cox
Photographer: Antonis Achilleos, Jen Causey
Prop Stylists: Buffy Hargett Miller, Lydia Pursell
Food Stylists: Ruth Blackburn, Margaret Monroe Dickey, Ali Ramee

PRINT PRODUCTION:
WATERBURY PUBLICATIONS, INC.

Library of Congress Control Number: 2023934788

ISBN-13: 978-1-4197-7251-1

First Edition 2023
Printed in the United States of America
10 9 8 7 6 5 4 3 2 1
Call 1-800-826-4707 for more information

Distributed in 2023 by Abrams, an imprint of ABRAMS.
Abrams® is a registered trademark of Harry N. Abrams, Inc.

ABRAMS The Art of Books
195 Broadway, New York, NY 10007
abramsbooks.com

Holiday Planner

Get a jump start on your holiday to-do list with this helpful planner. Create guest lists, keep track of gifts for family and friends, and stay on top of all the details for an organized, low-stress holiday.

PLANNING CALENDAR FOR NOVEMBER

HOLIDAY HOTLINES

PLANNING CALENDAR FOR DECEMBER

DECORATING PLANNER

CHRISTMAS TREE 101

PARTY PLANNER

CHRISTMAS DINNER PLANNER

GIFTS & GREETINGS

HOLIDAY MEMORIES

LOOKING AHEAD

November 2023

SUNDAY	MONDAY	TUESDAY	WEDNESDAY
			Time to invite Thanksgiving guests, plan the menu, and make a shopping list. **1**
Daylight saving time ends at 2 a.m. Turn clocks back an hour for extra rest! **5**	Order your fresh turkey now. **6**	Set out serving pieces you plan to use. Attach sticky notes to label what will go in each. **7**	Take inventory of pots, pans, and baking dishes. Buy or borrow any needed. **8**
Need a kids' table? Wrap a small table with kraft paper and provide crayons. **12**	Clean and organize the fridge. **13**	Take stock. Buy nonperishables in bulk like nuts and dried fruit to save. **14**	Tidy the least-used rooms in the house, which are less likely to get messy again. **15**
Shop for perishable grocery items such as milk, cheese, and produce. **19**	Serving a frozen turkey? Allow 1 day to thaw in the fridge for every 4 lb. of bird. **20**	Get fired up! Clean the fireplace and take stock of candles and votives. **21**	Buy fresh flowers and other perishables needed to assemble centerpieces. **22**
Throwing a holiday party? Send invites now. Calendars fill fast! **26**	Online shoppers, start clicking! Cyber Monday is here. **27**	Free up space in your coat closet, and vacuum and dust the entry. **28**	Make a merry holiday playlist. **29**

THURSDAY	FRIDAY	SATURDAY
Tackle home repairs and tidy up in advance of guests. **2**	Light an autumn-inspired candle for a lovely "scentsation" to get in the spirit. **3**	Ask friends and family for gift ideas to start your holiday shopping plan early. **4**
Plan your centerpiece and table setting. **9**	Order holiday cards and update your address list (page 189). **10**	Confirm head count for Thanksgiving dinner. **11**
Round up board games, playing cards, and photo albums to entertain guests while you're busy in the kitchen. **16**	Iron linens, polish the silver, and wash glassware and dishes. **17**	Make a prep list for each dish. Spread tasks from now through Thanksgiving Day. **18**
Happy Thanksgiving! Say "yes" to offers of help from guests so you can enjoy the day. **Thanksgiving 23**	Shoppers, start your engines— it's Black Friday! **24**	Enjoy those Thanksgiving leftovers. **25**
Gather recipes, plan Christmas menus (page 56), and clip coupons. **30**		

Holiday Hotlines

Use these toll-free numbers when you have last-minute food questions.

USDA Meat & Poultry Hotline:
1-888-674-6854

FDA Center for Food Safety:
1-888-723-3366

Butterball Turkey Talk Line:
1-800-BUTTERBALL

Butterball Turkey Text Line:
1-844-877-3456

Jennie-O Turkey Hotline:
1-800-TURKEYS

Ocean Spray
Holiday Helpline:
1-800-662-3263

Fleischmann's Yeast
Baker Hotline:
1-800-777-4959

December 2023

SUNDAY	MONDAY	TUESDAY	WEDNESDAY
Purchase stamps, gift wrap, tags, ribbons, tape, and scissors. **3**	Plan gifts (page 188) and decorating projects (page 182). **4**	Make cookie dough and freeze, or bake cookies and cakes and freeze unfrosted (page 156). **5**	Send out holiday cards. Don't wait until post office lines grow. **6**
Fill bird feeders with seed for overwintering songbirds. **10**	Hang wreaths, drape the mantel, display cards, and dust off Christmas accents for weeks of enjoyment. **11**	Water your fresh Christmas tree. **12**	Make a gingerbread house! Bake and decorate holiday cookies to give neighbors, friends, and colleagues. **13**
Simmer cloves, allspice, a cinnamon stick, and an orange half in water to festively scent your home. **17**	Bundle up and head out to go caroling or enjoy the Christmas lights. **18**	Practice self-care. Treat yourself to a hot bath, coffee with a friend, or a nap. **19**	Watch your favorite holiday film by a roaring fire. **20**
Prepare an elegant Homecoming Feast (page 80). **Christmas Eve 24**	Merry Christmas! Enjoy an easy Merry Brunchmas (page 58). **Christmas Day 25**	Go for a family walk, bike, or hike. **Boxing Day 26**	Plan your goals, intentions, or resolutions for the year ahead. **27**

THURSDAY	FRIDAY	SATURDAY	
	Visit the tree lot to pick your tree or unpack the faux fir.	Test the Christmas lights and replace fuses or strands.	
	....	....	....
	....	....	....
	....	....	....
	....	....	....
	1	**2**	....
Give back: Deliver meals, donate to a cause, visit the sick or homebound.	Check expiration dates on unused gift cards and use them to buy gifts for others.	Go natural and dehydrate citrus slices for pretty ornaments or cocktail garnishes.	....
....	....	....	....
....	....	....	....
....	....	....	....
7	**8**	**9**	....
Get tickets to holiday performances at the theater or symphony hall.	Finalize online purchases today before shipping prices jump.	Show teachers, the mail carrier, a babysitter, or colleagues appreciation with a small gift.	....
....	....	....	....
....	....	....	....
....	....	....	....
14	**15**	**16**	....
It's the first day of winter—days will start to get longer again!	Invite friends and loved ones for a casual Ho Ho Hoedown (page 70).	Don't forget the stocking stuffers!	....
....	....	....	....
....	....	....	....
....	....	....	....
Winter Solstice 21	**22**	**23**	**SUNDAY**
Phone loved ones you missed this holiday.	Return or exchange any gifts before return deadlines.	Get a jump start on your thank-you notes.	Host a super simple "App-y" New Year party (page 94) to ring in 2024!
....	....	....	....
....	....	....	....
....	....	....	....
28	**29**	**30**	**New Year's Eve 31**

Decorating Planner

Here's a list of details and finishing touches you can use
to tailor a picture-perfect house this holiday season.

Decorative materials needed

FROM THE YARD ....

FROM AROUND THE HOUSE ....

FROM THE STORE ....

OTHER ....

Holiday decorations

FOR THE TABLE ....

FOR THE DOOR ....

FOR THE MANTEL ....

FOR THE STAIRCASE ....

OTHER..

Create a Decorator's Toolkit

Our photo stylists guard their toolkits like the family jewels. A well-stocked kit means
you have just what you need at the ready to get you through the holidays and beyond.

- ☐ Tools (hammer, screwdrivers, clamps)
- ☐ Nails, screws, S-hooks, tacks
- ☐ Adhesive strips and hooks
- ☐ Staple gun and staples
- ☐ Hot-glue gun and glue sticks
- ☐ Crafts glue
- ☐ Superglue
- ☐ Clothespins
- ☐ Funnel
- ☐ Tape measure
- ☐ Twine

- ☐ Fishing line
- ☐ Green florists wire
- ☐ Sewing kit
- ☐ Lint roller
- ☐ Steamer or iron
- ☐ Paint brushes (assorted)
- ☐ Scissors
- ☐ Floral snips
- ☐ Lighter
- ☐ Batteries (assorted)
- ☐ Fuses for Christmas lights
- ☐ Gift-wrapping tape

- ☐ Double-sided tape
- ☐ Painters tape
- ☐ Museum Wax
- ☐ Putty
- ☐ Adhesive remover
- ☐ WD-40
- ☐ Window cleaner
- ☐ Furniture polish
- ☐ Touch-up paint
- ☐ Static duster
- ☐ Stain-remover stick

Christmas Tree 101

Follow these steps to finding your perfect match.

KNOW YOUR MAXIMUM SIZE

Calculate your maximum tree size: Measure the height of your ceiling and subtract
1 foot. This allows ample room for your topper. Keep in mind that the smaller the room, the
skinnier the tree should be.

CHECK FOR FRESHNESS ON THE LOT

Run your fingers down a branch before you buy. All needles should remain intact, and your
hand should smell like your evergreen of choice. Gentle shaking should result in very little
needle drop. Even with diligent care, cut trees only last a couple of weeks. Your best bet is
to cut your own from a farm or purchase one from a store or lot that offers trees harvested
within days of delivery. True fir trees typically last the longest, according to Rick Bates,
Professor of Horticulture at Pennsylvania State University. In the east that means Fraser
fir, and in the west, Noble fir.

RECUT THE TRUNK

Once home, you're probably ready to decorate—but not before recutting the trunk about
1 inch above the butt end to aid in water absorption. If you don't have a saw, most tree lots
will do this for you.

WATER OFTEN

Get your tree into a bucket of water within an hour of cutting, or the pores will seal with
sap and your effort will be in vain. If the tree is fresh-cut from a farm, put it in the stand.
Otherwise, soak it in a bucket of water outside overnight. You can also spray it down with a
hose to remove debris and help hydrate the needles.

KEEP FRUIT AWAY

"What?" you say. It's true: Just like a banana can help an avocado ripen more quickly, the
ethylene gas released by fruit will hasten needle drop from a tree's branches. So don't put
the fruit basket beneath the tree...or perhaps a tree in your kitchen.

Party Planner

Stay on top of your party plans with this time-saving menu organizer.

GUESTS	WHAT THEY'RE BRINGING	SERVING PIECES NEEDED
....	☐ appetizer ☐ beverage ☐ bread ☐ main dish ☐ side dish ☐ dessert	....
....	☐ appetizer ☐ beverage ☐ bread ☐ main dish ☐ side dish ☐ dessert	....
....	☐ appetizer ☐ beverage ☐ bread ☐ main dish ☐ side dish ☐ dessert	....
....	☐ appetizer ☐ beverage ☐ bread ☐ main dish ☐ side dish ☐ dessert	....
....	☐ appetizer ☐ beverage ☐ bread ☐ main dish ☐ side dish ☐ dessert	....
....	☐ appetizer ☐ beverage ☐ bread ☐ main dish ☐ side dish ☐ dessert	....
....	☐ appetizer ☐ beverage ☐ bread ☐ main dish ☐ side dish ☐ dessert	....
....	☐ appetizer ☐ beverage ☐ bread ☐ main dish ☐ side dish ☐ dessert	....
....	☐ appetizer ☐ beverage ☐ bread ☐ main dish ☐ side dish ☐ dessert	....
....	☐ appetizer ☐ beverage ☐ bread ☐ main dish ☐ side dish ☐ dessert	....
....	☐ appetizer ☐ beverage ☐ bread ☐ main dish ☐ side dish ☐ dessert	....
....	☐ appetizer ☐ beverage ☐ bread ☐ main dish ☐ side dish ☐ dessert	....
....	☐ appetizer ☐ beverage ☐ bread ☐ main dish ☐ side dish ☐ dessert	....
....	☐ appetizer ☐ beverage ☐ bread ☐ main dish ☐ side dish ☐ dessert	....
....	☐ appetizer ☐ beverage ☐ bread ☐ main dish ☐ side dish ☐ dessert	....
....	☐ appetizer ☐ beverage ☐ bread ☐ main dish ☐ side dish ☐ dessert	....

Party Guest List

Party To-Do List

Christmas Dinner Planner

Use this space to create a menu, to-do list, and guest list for your special holiday celebration.

Menu Ideas

....
....
....
....
....
....
....

Dinner To-Do List

....
....
....
....
....
....
....

Christmas Dinner Guest List

....
....
....
....
....
....
....
....
....

Pantry List

Grocery List

Gifts & Greetings

Keep up with family and friends' sizes, jot down gift ideas, and record purchases in this convenient chart. Also use it to keep track of addresses for your Christmas card list.

Gift List and Size Charts

	GIFT PURCHASED/MADE	SENT
jeans____ shirt____ sweater____ jacket____ shoes____ belt____ blouse____ skirt____ slacks____ dress____ suit____ coat____ pajamas____ robe____ hat____ gloves____ ring____		
jeans____ shirt____ sweater____ jacket____ shoes____ belt____ blouse____ skirt____ slacks____ dress____ suit____ coat____ pajamas____ robe____ hat____ gloves____ ring____		
jeans____ shirt____ sweater____ jacket____ shoes____ belt____ blouse____ skirt____ slacks____ dress____ suit____ coat____ pajamas____ robe____ hat____ gloves____ ring____		
jeans____ shirt____ sweater____ jacket____ shoes____ belt____ blouse____ skirt____ slacks____ dress____ suit____ coat____ pajamas____ robe____ hat____ gloves____ ring____		
jeans____ shirt____ sweater____ jacket____ shoes____ belt____ blouse____ skirt____ slacks____ dress____ suit____ coat____ pajamas____ robe____ hat____ gloves____ ring____		
jeans____ shirt____ sweater____ jacket____ shoes____ belt____ blouse____ skirt____ slacks____ dress____ suit____ coat____ pajamas____ robe____ hat____ gloves____ ring____		
jeans____ shirt____ sweater____ jacket____ shoes____ belt____ blouse____ skirt____ slacks____ dress____ suit____ coat____ pajamas____ robe____ hat____ gloves____ ring____		

Christmas Card List

NAME	ADDRESS	SENT

Holiday Memories

Hold on to priceless Christmas memories forever with handwritten
recollections of this season's magical moments.

Treasured Traditions

Keep track of your family's favorite holiday customs and pastimes on these lines.

....

....

....

....

....

....

....

....

....

....

....

....

Special Holiday Activities

What holiday events do you look forward to year after year? Write them down here.

....

....

....

....

....

....

....

....

....

....

Holiday Visits and Visitors

Keep a list of this year's holiday visitors.
Jot down friend and family news as well.

....
....
....
....
....
....
....
....
....
....
....
....
....
....
....
....
....
....
....
....
....
....
....
....
....
....

This Year's Favorite Recipes

APPETIZERS AND BEVERAGES

....
....
....
....
....

ENTRÉES ....

....
....
....

SIDES AND SALADS ....

....
....
....

COOKIES AND CANDIES ....

....
....
....

DESSERTS ....

....
....
....

Looking Ahead

Holiday Wrap-up

Use this checklist to record thank-you notes sent for holiday gifts and hospitality.

NAME	GIFT AND/OR EVENT	NOTE SENT
....	....	☐
....	....	☐
....	....	☐
....	....	☐
....	....	☐
....	....	☐
....	....	☐
....	....	☐
....	....	☐
....	....	☐
....	....	☐
....	....	☐
....	....	☐

Notes for Next Year

Write down your ideas for Christmas 2024 on the lines below.

....

....

....

....

....

....

....

....

....

....

....

....